JAMIE OLIVER

Easy Air Fryer

Photography DAVID LOFTUS

Design JAMES VERITY

FLATIRON
BOOKS
NEW YORK

Contents

We all love air fryers

As I write this, here in the UK alone more than 50% of households own an air fryer. As I saw their popularity grow, I knew I wanted to find out exactly why these machines are taking over our kitchens. Writing cookbooks, for me, is all about responding to what you, the public, are asking for, so I've gone down a bit of an air-fryer rabbit hole, experimenting at length with these convenient cooking machines to find out just what they can do. If air fryers are getting more people to give cooking a go, then that can only be a good thing. And believe me, they really are rather brilliant.

They're super-versatile . . .

It's not all just about crispy fries and spuds, though of course those things are delicious given the air-fryer treatment (check out my Really good roasted potatoes, page 103). But what I've found most exciting is just how much you can actually cook in them. From soups and salads, to pasta bakes, burgers, fish dishes, bread and desserts, there's so much potential there. That's exactly what I've tried to bottle in this book, pushing the boundaries of what the air fryer can do to create easy dishes that deliver big on flavor and texture, and that hopefully will surprise and delight you in what you can achieve!

. . . and a great bit of equipment

Think of your air fryer as another tool in your kitchen arsenal. It's there to work for you, and has already earned its place alongside the oven, stove and microwave. I hope the wide range of recipes here will inspire you to think a bit differently about your machine – whether you're an air-fryer novice or in need of new ideas, let this book start you on your journey to new air-fryer territory. You're going to love it!

How an air fryer works

Air fryers allow for quick, efficient, relatively hands-off cooking. They blast food with hot dry air so it becomes crisp and golden (like it's been fried, but it hasn't!).

Air fryers are essentially a heating element with a fan above it that blows air down into a removable drawer (also called a basket). The hot air is blown around the food in the drawer, cooking and crisping it on all sides. Each drawer has a removable shelf (also called a grid) that can be utilized in different ways, which you'll see in these recipes. Unless directed to remove it, all recipes use the air fryer with the shelf in place.

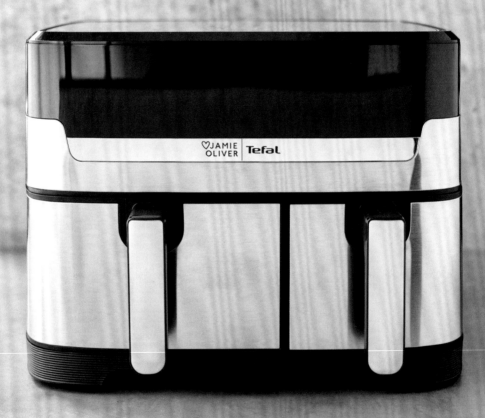

You can often cook stuff in less time than it takes for the oven to heat up, and generally things cook a bit more quickly, or, you can cook things you'd normally do on the stove in a much more hands-off way. Air fryers are quite compact and energy-efficient, so they're ideal when you just want to cook a portion of something without turning the oven on, hopefully helping you to save a bit of money, too.

Easy Air Fryer pantry

As with all my recent books, I always presume you've got these five staple ingredients. They pop up regularly throughout this book and aren't included in each individual ingredients list. The five heroes are olive oil for cooking; extra virgin olive oil for dressing and finishing dishes; red wine vinegar as a good all-rounder when it comes to acidity and balancing marinades, sauces and dressings; and, of course, sea salt and black pepper for seasoning to perfection.

Let's chat equipment

I tend to use a small range of equipment on repeat, so don't feel like you need to spend a fortune to get equipped in the kitchen. As well as your air fryer, there are a handful of things that will set you up well. A cutting board and decent knife is a given for nearly every recipe. And when it comes to making your life easier, a vegetable peeler, box grater and mortar and pestle are all fantastic for creating texture and boosting flavor. A blender or immersion blender and a food processor will always be a bonus, too. I'm also really into using a spritzer for olive oil these days – it makes it easier to control your oil use, both in terms of where it goes and the amount you use, helping you to be healthier, too.

Tasty lunch and dinner plates you can have on the table in no time

Quick
fixes

Feta & tomato pasta

 Serves 4   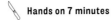 Hands on 7 minutes   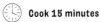 Cook 15 minutes   1 Drawer

1 lb (generous 3 cups) ripe mixed-color cherry tomatoes

2 cloves of garlic

1 fresh red chili

6 kalamata olives, with pits

½ a bunch of basil (about ½ oz)

4 oz feta cheese

12 oz orecchiette or your favorite dried pasta

1 Halve the tomatoes, peel and thinly slice the garlic, halve and slice the chili (seed if you like), smash, pit and tear up the olives, then place it all in the air-fryer drawer. Finely chop the basil stems, reserving the leaves, and sprinkle into the drawer. Add 2 tablespoons of olive oil, ½ tablespoon of red wine vinegar and a pinch each of sea salt and black pepper, and toss to coat.

2 Break the feta into the drawer in 3 pieces, stacking them on top of each other, and cook it all for 15 minutes at 400°F, or until the tomatoes are jammy and the feta is golden and soft.

3 Meanwhile, cook the pasta in a pot of boiling salted water according to the package instructions. Use a slotted spoon to transfer the pasta straight into the drawer of tomatoes, tear in most of the basil leaves and toss together, then season to perfection, loosening with a splash of cooking water, if needed.

4 Divide between bowls, sprinkle with the remaining basil leaves, and finish with a little extra virgin olive oil, if you like.

ENERGY	FAT	SAT FAT	PROTEIN	CARBS	SUGARS	SALT	FIBER
424kcal	14.9g	5.5g	14.9g	61.5g	5.8g	1.4g	1.3g

Punchy Welsh rarebit

 Serves 2    Hands on 7 minutes    Cook 10 minutes   1 Drawer

2 large slices of good bread
(about ¾ inch thick)

1 egg

2 oz Cheddar cheese

1 tbsp crème fraîche

1 heaping tsp English
or Dijon mustard

¼ cup jarred sliced jalapeños

1 Granny Smith apple

1 little gem lettuce

optional: Worcestershire sauce

1   Place the bread in the air-fryer drawer and toast for 5 minutes at 400°F.

2   Whisk the egg in a bowl until light and foamy, then finely grate in the cheese, add the crème fraîche, mustard and a pinch of black pepper, and mix well.

3   Remove the bread from the air fryer, flip over, spoon the rarebit mixture over both pieces, then gently poke in the jalapeño slices. Return to the drawer and cook for 5 minutes at 400°F, or until golden and bubbling.

4   While it cooks, thinly slice the apple into rounds, then across into matchsticks. Separate out the lettuce leaves, thinly slice the core, and slice the inner tender leaves. Gently toss it all in a little extra virgin olive oil, red wine vinegar, sea salt and pepper. Plate up with the rarebit, add a shake of Worcestershire sauce, if you like, and enjoy!

Easy swaps

Feel free to swap in any good melty cheese of your choice. Gruyère, Swiss, Comté and Fontina would all work well here. Some of my Great British faves are Westcombe Cheddar, Lincolnshire Poacher and Mrs. Kirkham's Lancashire. Adding jalapeños gives a punchy flavor hit, but you can swap in all sorts of flavor bombs here – try a layer of chili jam or red pepper jelly, chutney or even sweet pickle relish under the rarebit mixture.

ENERGY	FAT	SAT FAT	PROTEIN	CARBS	SUGARS	SALT	FIBER
341kcal	19.6g	9g	14.4g	26.9g	9.6g	1.8g	2.8g

Springtime salmon in a bag

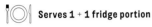 Serves 1 + 1 fridge portion   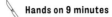 Hands on 9 minutes   Cook 15 minutes   1 Drawer

1 x 8½-oz package of cooked rice

8 oz asparagus

1 cup freshly podded or frozen peas

1 lemon

1 tsp Dijon mustard

3 tbsp plain yogurt

2 x 5-oz salmon or trout fillets, skin on, scaled, pin-boned

2 sprigs of mint

optional: 2 tbsp dry white wine

1 We're going to make two parcels – you can either cook them one after the other or you can pop one into the fridge raw, where it will keep happily for up to 2 days, ready to cook to order. So tear off two large sheets of heavy-duty aluminum foil (about 24 inches long), fold each in half, then open up like a book.

2 Tip the rice into a bowl and break it up. Snap the woody ends off the asparagus and slice the stalks, leaving the tips whole, then add to the bowl along with the peas. Finely grate in the lemon zest, add 1 tablespoon of olive oil and a pinch each of sea salt and black pepper, and mix well.

3 Divide the rice mixture between the two sheets of foil, placing it on just one half of each piece. Mix the mustard and yogurt together, spoon it over the rice, then lightly season the salmon and place it on top, skin-side down.

4 Pick the mint leaves, reserving the nice baby ones, then thinly slice the rest and sprinkle over the salmon. Fold over the foil to create a parcel, twisting the edges to seal and adding the wine or 2 tablespoons of water before sealing the final side.

5 Place one parcel in the air-fryer drawer and cook for 15 minutes at 400°F, or until the salmon is just cooked through. Carefully tear open the foil, sprinkle with the reserved baby mint leaves and serve with lemon wedges.

ENERGY	FAT	SAT FAT	PROTEIN	CARBS	SUGARS	SALT	FIBER
503kcal	17.7g	3.8g	39.3g	48.9g	5.9g	1.2g	7.7g

Smoked mackerel on toast

 Serves 2    Hands on 10 minutes   Cook 10 minutes   1 Drawer

6 oz smoked mackerel or smoked trout fillets

2 slices of focaccia or bread of your choice

1 x 14½-oz can of peeled new potatoes (or 10 oz of peeled, cooked potatoes)

1 tsp English or Dijon mustard

⅔ cup plain yogurt

2 tsp drained capers

½ a bunch of chives (about ⅓ oz)

1 pickle

1 vine-ripe tomato (6 oz)

½ an English cucumber

½ a lemon

1 Place the mackerel fillets skin-side down on the focaccia slices, then place in the air-fryer drawer and cook for 10 minutes at 400°F, or until golden.

2 Drain the potatoes, chopping any larger ones, and place in a large bowl with the mustard, yogurt and capers. Finely chop the chives and add most to the bowl. Thinly slice the pickle, chop the tomato and roughly chop the cucumber, add it all, mix well, and season to perfection with sea salt and black pepper.

3 Divide the salad between plates, then add the crispy mackerel on toast. Carefully pour any cooking juices from the drawer over the top, and finish with the remaining chives. Serve with lemon wedges.

ENERGY	FAT	SAT FAT	PROTEIN	CARBS	SUGARS	SALT	FIBER
498kcal	25.9g	7g	26.7g	38.5g	9.9g	2.8g	3.8g

Creamy garlic mussels

 Serves 1    Hands on 7 minutes   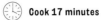 Cook 17 minutes   2 Drawer

1 shallot

2 cloves of garlic

1½ tbsp unsalted butter

5 tbsp dry white wine

1 x 4-inch piece of French baguette (about 2 oz)

¼ of a bunch of chives (about ¼ oz)

1 lb mussels, scrubbed, debearded

2 tbsp crème fraîche

1 Remove the shelf from the large air-fryer drawer. Peel and finely chop the shallot and garlic, place in the drawer with the butter and cook for 12 minutes at 350°F, or until softened, shaking halfway through and adding the wine.

2 Meanwhile, thinly slice the baguette on the bias and place in the small drawer for 8 minutes at 400°F, or until golden and crisp. Finely chop the chives.

3 Check the mussels – tap any open ones and, if they don't close, discard them. Scatter into the large drawer and cook for 5 minutes at 400°F, or until the mussels have opened and are soft and juicy. Discard any that remain closed.

4 Toss the crème fraîche and most of the chives with the mussels, then season to perfection with sea salt and black pepper. Place the crispy toasts in a serving bowl, tip over the mussels and all those tasty juices, sprinkle with the remaining chives, and dig in!

ENERGY	FAT	SAT FAT	PROTEIN	CARBS	SUGARS	SALT	FIBER
574kcal	31g	19.1g	25.3g	34g	3.7g	1.5g	2.1g

Yes for yogurt flatbread!

Just 10 minutes in the air fryer creates perfect flatbreads. With an even, crunchy exterior and a lovely soft interior, what's not to love?

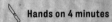 **Hands on 4 minutes**   **Cook 10 minutes**   **1 Drawer**

Simply mix together **1 cup of self-rising flour (or 1 cup of all-purpose flour plus 1½ teaspoons baking powder and a second pinch of salt)**, a good pinch of sea salt, **a scant ½ cup of plain yogurt** and 1 tablespoon of olive oil, using your hands when it becomes too hard to mix with a fork. Knead for 1 minute, then stretch and pat the dough out to ½ inch thick, making sure it's no bigger than your air-fryer drawer. Leave as is, or lightly press **½ teaspoon of cumin, fennel or nigella seeds** into the surface on both sides. Place in the drawer and cook for 10 minutes at 400°F, or until golden and puffed up, turning halfway.

Black bean veg & tofu

 Serves 2   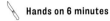 Hands on 6 minutes   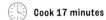 Cook 17 minutes   2 Drawer

4 scallions

12 oz crunchy veg, such as bell peppers, carrots, broccoli, green beans, snow peas and sugar snap peas

10 oz extra-firm tofu

2 heaping tbsp black bean sauce

12 oz fresh thick udon noodles (or cooked, drained udon noodles)

1 lime

1 tbsp runny honey

2 tbsp unsalted roasted peanuts

4 sprigs of cilantro

1 Remove the shelf from the large air-fryer drawer. Trim the scallions and chop into 1-inch lengths. Trim and prep the crunchy veg, slicing into bite-size pieces. Scatter it all into the drawer, spritz with olive oil, season with sea salt and black pepper and toss to coat. Cook for 10 minutes at 350°F, or until starting to char, shaking halfway.

2 Pat the tofu dry with paper towels, then chop into ¾-inch chunks, place in the small drawer and toss with half the black bean sauce and 1 teaspoon of oil. Shake into an even layer and cook for 10 minutes at 400°F, shaking halfway.

3 When the time's up on the veg, separate the noodles, toss with a spritz of oil, then scatter into the large drawer. Cook for 3 minutes at 350°F while, in a small bowl, you mix together the remaining black bean sauce, 2 tablespoons of water and the juice of ½ a lime. Pour over the noodles and veg, toss well and cook for a final 2 minutes at 350°F. Drizzle the honey over the tofu, toss to coat and cook for a final 2 minutes at 350°F, or until sticky.

4 Plate up the noodles and veg, top with the tofu, crush and sprinkle on the peanuts, pick over the cilantro leaves and serve with lime wedges.

ENERGY	FAT	SAT FAT	PROTEIN	CARBS	SUGARS	SALT	FIBER
594kcal	18.6g	2.8g	27.8g	67.8g	18.7g	1.5g	7.6g

Spiced fish & rice bake

 Serves 1    Hands on 5 minutes    Cook 15 minutes   1 Drawer

6 tbsp basmati rice

1 tsp of your favorite curry paste

1 heaping tsp mango chutney

3 oz (about ¾ cup) ripe cherry tomatoes

4 sprigs of cilantro

1 x 5-oz skinless white fish fillet, pin-boned

1 Place the rice in a small loaf pan that will fit inside the drawer of your air fryer. Add the curry paste and mango chutney, then halve and add the tomatoes. Finely chop and add the cilantro stems, reserving the leaves. Season with sea salt and black pepper, pour in a scant ½ cup of boiling water and mix well. Place the fish on top, season and drizzle with a little olive oil.

2 Cover the pan tightly with aluminum foil, place in the drawer and cook for 15 minutes at 400°F, then let rest in the drawer for another 5 minutes, or until the fish and rice are cooked through.

3 Spoon the fish and rice onto a plate and top with the reserved cilantro leaves. Nice served with a dollop of yogurt drizzled with a little extra virgin olive oil, if you like, and a lemon wedge.

ENERGY	FAT	SAT FAT	PROTEIN	CARBS	SUGARS	SALT	FIBER
454kcal	6.8g	0.9g	31.2g	71.2g	7.9g	1.2g	2.5g

Tasty toast toppers

The air fryer allows you to load up toast with wonderful things for very pleasing results. Here are a few of my favorite combos, all using cottage cheese as a vehicle for bigger flavor – I can't wait to see yours!

 **Hands on 6 minutes**   **Cook 7 minutes**   **1 Drawer**

Preheat your air fryer for 2 minutes to 400°F. Place **1 thick slice of bread** in the drawer – use seeded, sourdough, or whatever you like. Toast for 5 minutes at 400°F, flipping halfway, then rub the top with the cut side of **½ a clove of garlic**. Now, choose and load up one of the following combos, cook for 2 minutes at 400°F, or until melted, season to perfection with sea salt and black pepper and enjoy.

Topping combos

Mix **½ tablespoon of sun-dried tomato paste** with **1 tablespoon of cottage cheese**, spread on the toast, top with **2 slices of mozzarella** and finish with torn **basil leaves**.

Mix **½ tablespoon of harissa paste** with **1 tablespoon of cottage cheese**, spread on the toast, and top with **ripe avocado**, a little **feta cheese** and a pinch of **smoked paprika**.

Spread the toast with **½ teaspoon of Marmite**, mix **1 tablespoon each of grated sharp Cheddar and cottage cheese** with some chopped **pickled onions**, spread on the toast and crumble on **sour cream and onion potato chips**.

Think big hitters and flavors you know and love, reimagined in the air fryer

New classics

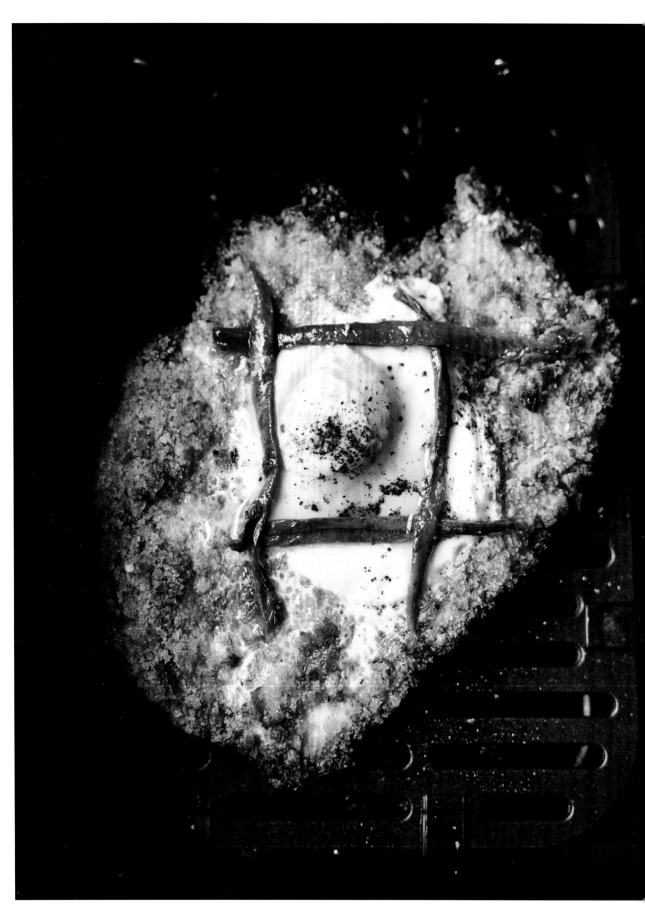

Chicken schnitzel

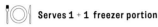 **Serves 1 + 1 freezer portion**   **Hands on 10 minutes**   **Cook 12 minutes**   **1 Drawer**

2 x 5-oz boneless, skinless chicken breasts

2 tbsp all-purpose flour

2 eggs

1 tbsp sun-dried tomato paste

2 large slices of stale white sandwich bread (about 3½ oz)

2 anchovy fillets in oil

½ a lemon

1 This method is perfect for one, as the pounded chicken fills the air-fryer drawer, but we're prepping two, as it's worthwhile – you can wrap the second one at the end of step 4 and pop it into the fridge for up to 3 days, or the freezer for up to 3 months.

2 Carefully slice into the chicken breasts horizontally, then open each one up flat like a book. One at a time, pound and flatten between two sheets of parchment paper to ¼ inch thick, then dust all over with the flour.

3 Beat 1 egg and the tomato paste in a shallow bowl, then season with sea salt and black pepper. In a food processor, blitz the bread with 1 tablespoon of olive oil into fine crumbs, then spread onto a plate.

4 Preheat the air fryer for 2 minutes to 400°F. Dip the floured chicken into the egg mixture, letting any excess drip off, then coat in the breadcrumbs, spending a bit of time really patting them on.

5 Spritz the piece of breaded chicken you are cooking now with oil, place in the drawer and cook for 4 minutes, or until golden (8 minutes from frozen). Flip and cook for 3 minutes, then flip again, crack 1 egg on top, and cook for a final 5 minutes, or until the egg is cooked to your liking and the chicken is cooked through.

6 Plate up, then thinly slice the anchovies lengthwise and lay over the schnitzel. Serve with a lemon wedge. Great with potato salad and dressed salad greens.

ENERGY	FAT	SAT FAT	PROTEIN	CARBS	SUGARS	SALT	FIBER
482kcal	15.6g	3.6g	51.2g	35.1g	1.9g	1.8g	2g

Lamb kofta

 Serves 2   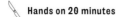 Hands on 20 minutes    Cook 20 minutes   1 Drawer

½ cup whole wheat couscous

1 lemon

1 oz dried apricots (about 4 pieces)

3 tbsp shelled unsalted pistachios

8 oz ground lamb

1 tsp ras el hanout

½ a small red onion

½ a bunch of Italian parsley (about ½ oz)

½ a bunch of mint (about ½ oz)

1 x 15-oz can of chickpeas

1 tbsp harissa paste

¼ cup Greek yogurt

1 Put the couscous into a bowl, finely grate in the lemon zest, just cover with boiling water, cover and set aside.

2 Finely chop the apricots and pistachios and put into another bowl with the lamb, ras el hanout and a good pinch each of sea salt and black pepper. Once the couscous has absorbed all the liquid, fluff up with a fork, add one-third to the lamb mixture, then massage together with clean hands.

3 Divide the mixture into 8 equal pieces, then shape into koftas with your fingertips, leaving dents in the surface to increase the gnarly caramelized bits as they cook. Place in the air-fryer drawer, spritz with olive oil and cook for 20 minutes at 350°F, or until sizzling, shaking halfway.

4 Meanwhile, peel and very thinly slice the red onion, then massage with a pinch of salt and 2 tablespoons of red wine vinegar and let sit to quickly pickle.

5 Finely chop the herb leaves and add to the remaining couscous with a good squeeze of lemon juice and 1 tablespoon of extra virgin olive oil. Drain and add the chickpeas, toss well, season to perfection and divide between plates.

6 Place the kofta on top, then ripple the harissa through the yogurt and spoon on the side. Top with the pickled red onions and serve with lemon wedges.

ENERGY	FAT	SAT FAT	PROTEIN	CARBS	SUGARS	SALT	FIBER
721kcal	32.8g	9.3g	43.4g	64.4g	10.5g	1g	12.4g

Chili con carne meatballs

 Serves 2   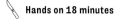 **Hands on 18 minutes**    **Cook 25 minutes**   **1 Drawer**

1 sweet potato (about 8 oz)

2 tsp smoked paprika

1 x 15-oz can of black beans

2 tsp cumin seeds

1 fresh red chili

½ a bunch of cilantro (about ½ oz)

8 oz ground beef

1 lime

8 oz (about 1½ cups) ripe cherry tomatoes

chipotle hot sauce

1 Wash the sweet potato, chop into ¾-inch chunks, then, in a bowl, toss with the paprika, 1 tablespoon of olive oil, and a pinch each of sea salt and black pepper.

2 Remove the shelf from the air-fryer drawer, tip in the beans, juice and all, add 1 teaspoon of cumin seeds, and season well. Replace the shelf, add the sweet potato, reserving the bowl for later, and cook for 15 minutes at 350°F.

3 To make the balls, finely chop the chili (seed, if you like) and most of the cilantro, stems and all, reserving a few nice leaves. Scrape into the empty bowl with the remaining cumin seeds and the ground beef, finely grate in the lime zest, season, then massage together with clean hands.

4 Divide the mixture into 10 equal balls, then add to the drawer with the tomatoes, shake into an even layer, and cook for 10 minutes at 350°F, or until lightly golden and cooked through, shaking halfway.

5 Remove the balls, sweet potato and tomatoes to a plate and use tongs to carefully remove the shelf. Squeeze half the lime juice into the beans, add a few shakes of hot sauce, then mash half the beans to create a creamier texture. Divide between plates, pile the balls, sweet potato and tomatoes on top and sprinkle with the reserved cilantro leaves. Serve with lime wedges and extra hot sauce, if you like.

ENERGY	FAT	SAT FAT	PROTEIN	CARBS	SUGARS	SALT	FIBER
462kcal	14.6g	3.9g	39.7g	39g	10.1g	1.5g	18g

Sweet chili shrimp burgers

 Serves 2   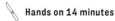 Hands on 14 minutes   Cook 12 minutes   1 Drawer

¾-inch piece of ginger

2 scallions

½ a bunch of cilantro
(about ½ oz)

½ cup drained canned
corn kernels

6 oz raw peeled jumbo shrimp

2 tbsp sweet red chili sauce

2 seeded burger buns

1 tbsp Greek yogurt

1 little gem lettuce

½ a lime

1 Peel the ginger, trim the scallions, then finely chop with the cilantro stems, reserving the leaves. Add the corn to the board along with the shrimp and a small pinch each of sea salt and black pepper, then keep chopping it all until fine but retaining a bit of texture. Smash and mix it all with the flat side of your knife for a couple of minutes, helping it to come together.

2 With wet hands, divide the mixture in half, then shape and pat into ¾-inch-thick patties. Place in the air-fryer drawer, spritz with olive oil, and cook for 10 minutes at 400°F, or until golden and cooked through.

3 Brush half the chili sauce over the burgers and cook for another 2 minutes at 400°F, adding the buns cut-side up alongside.

4 Mix the remaining chili sauce with the yogurt, remove the buns from the air fryer, and spread half the sauce on the bun bottoms, then place the burgers on top. Shred the lettuce, mix with the reserved cilantro leaves and the rest of the chili yogurt, pile on top of the burgers, squeeze on the lime, then press the bun tops on, serving any leftover salad on the side.

ENERGY	FAT	SAT FAT	PROTEIN	CARBS	SUGARS	SALT	FIBER
484kcal	14.3g	2.9g	19.3g	60.3g	15.7g	1.8g	5.4g

Loaded BBQ bean potato skins

 Serves 2   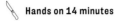 Hands on 14 minutes    Cook 47 minutes   2 Drawer

2 russet potatoes
(about 9 oz each)

1 x 15-oz can of cannellini
beans (also known as
white kidney beans)

2 tbsp ketchup

1 tbsp smoked paprika

½ tbsp runny honey

1 lemon

½ a bunch of chives
(about ⅓ oz)

2 oz melty cheese,
such as Cheddar

12 oz crunchy veg & fruit,
such as green cabbage,
carrots, fennel, apples
and pears

1   Wash the potatoes, prick a few times with a sharp knife, then rub each one with ½ teaspoon of olive oil and a pinch of sea salt. Place in the large air-fryer drawer and cook for 40 minutes at 350°F, or until soft, turning halfway.

2   Remove the shelf from the small drawer and tip in the beans, juice and all, ketchup, paprika and honey. Cook for 40 minutes at 350°F, stirring halfway.

3   Use tongs to transfer the soft potatoes to your board, halve lengthwise, then scoop out the fluffy centers, leaving ¼ inch of potato around the edges.

4   Mash up the fluffy centers and stir into the beans along with half the lemon juice. Finely chop the chives and add half to the beans, reserving the rest, then season to perfection with salt and black pepper. Spoon the mixture back into the potato skins, grate on the cheese, then return the loaded skins to the large drawer and cook for 7 minutes at 350°F, or until crispy and heated through.

5   Meanwhile, make a quick slaw by trimming and grating your chosen veg and fruit. Dress with the remaining lemon juice and ½ tablespoon of extra virgin olive oil, mix in the remaining chives, and season to perfection. Serve alongside the loaded potato skins.

ENERGY	FAT	SAT FAT	PROTEIN	CARBS	SUGARS	SALT	FIBER
592kcal	18g	6.6g	22.4g	73.5g	16.2g	1.3g	15.2g

Sesame chicken meatballs

 Serves 2   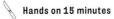 Hands on 15 minutes   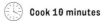 Cook 10 minutes   1 Drawer

1 fresh red chili

½ a bunch of cilantro
(about ½ oz)

2 cloves of garlic

¾-inch piece of ginger

2 x 5-oz boneless, skinless
chicken breasts

1 heaping tbsp peanut butter

1 tbsp reduced-sodium
soy sauce

3 tbsp toasted sesame seeds

2 nests of vermicelli rice
noodles (about 3 oz total)

1 small carrot

¼ of an English cucumber

2 limes

2 scallions

2 tbsp sweet red chili sauce

1 Roughly chop the chili (seed, if you like) and place in a food processor with the cilantro stems, reserving the leaves. Peel and add the garlic and ginger, blitz until finely chopped, then pulse in the chicken breasts, peanut butter and soy until combined but still retaining a little texture.

2 Put the sesame seeds on a plate. With wet hands, divide the mixture into 10 equal meatballs, then gently roll in the sesame seeds, patting them on to coat. Place the meatballs in the air-fryer drawer and cook for 10 minutes at 400°F, or until golden and cooked through, shaking halfway.

3 In a bowl, cover the noodles with boiling water and let sit to rehydrate, then drain. Peel the carrot and matchstick along with the cucumber, toss with the drained noodles and the juice of ½ a lime, then divide between serving bowls. Trim and thinly slice the scallions.

4 Squeeze the juice of 1 lime over the meatballs, drizzle with the chili sauce, add a pinch each of sea salt and black pepper, toss well, then spoon into the bowls. Sprinkle with the scallions and cilantro leaves, drizzle with a little extra chili sauce, if you like, and serve with lime wedges.

ENERGY	FAT	SAT FAT	PROTEIN	CARBS	SUGARS	SALT	FIBER
547kcal	15.9g	3.4g	45.6g	55.4g	14.1g	1.6g	3.9g

Teriyaki pork ribs

 Serves 2    **Hands on 6 minutes**    **Cook 55 minutes**   **1 Drawer**

3 tbsp sugar

3 tbsp reduced-sodium soy sauce

1 tbsp rice wine vinegar

¾-inch piece of ginger

1 clove of garlic

1 tbsp cornstarch

1 rack of baby back ribs (about 1¼ lb)

2 scallions

1 Remove the shelf from the air-fryer drawer and add the sugar, soy and vinegar, along with 1¼ cups of water. Peel and finely grate in the ginger and garlic, add the cornstarch and mix to combine, then replace the shelf.

2 Rub the rack of ribs with a little olive oil and a pinch of sea salt, then place it on the shelf (cut it in half to help it fit, if needed). Cook for 50 minutes at 325°F, or until the meat is tender and starting to get gnarly and caramelized.

3 Use tongs to carefully remove the shelf, tipping the ribs into the sauce, then turn the ribs to coat. Cook for another 5 minutes at 400°F, or until the sauce sets and darkens on the ribs and the surrounding sauce thickens, too.

4 Slice up the ribs, then trim, thinly slice and sprinkle on the scallions. Pour the remaining sauce into a bowl for dunking. Great served with sticky rice and zingy seasonal greens.

ENERGY	FAT	SAT FAT	PROTEIN	CARBS	SUGARS	SALT	FIBER
394kcal	19.4g	7.6g	28.4g	28g	23.6g	2.6g	0.3g

Gochujang chicken burgers

 Serves 2   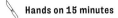 **Hands on 15 minutes**   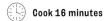 **Cook 16 minutes**   **1 Drawer**

2 boneless, skinless chicken thighs

2 tbsp all-purpose flour

1 egg

2 tbsp gochujang paste

2 medium slices of stale white sandwich bread (about 3 oz)

2 burger buns

12 oz crunchy veg, such as red cabbage, carrots, onions and radishes

1 fresh green chili

1 tbsp toasted sesame seeds

2 tbsp Greek yogurt

1 One at a time, pound and flatten the chicken thighs between two sheets of parchment paper to ½ inch thick, then dust all over with the flour.

2 Beat the egg with 1 tablespoon of gochujang in a shallow bowl, then season with sea salt and black pepper. In a food processor, blitz the bread with 1 tablespoon of olive oil into fine crumbs, then spread onto a plate.

3 Preheat the air fryer for 2 minutes to 400°F. Dip the floured chicken into the egg mixture, letting any excess drip off, then coat in the breadcrumbs, spending a bit of time really patting them on.

4 Evenly space the chicken in the air-fryer drawer and cook for 16 minutes, or until golden and cooked through, turning halfway and adding the buns cut-side up for the last 2 minutes.

5 Prep your veg, then finely shred or grate them to make a quick slaw – I use a vegetable peeler to create a super-fine, crunchy texture. Thinly slice and add the chili, along with the sesame seeds, 2 tablespoons of red wine vinegar and 1 tablespoon of extra virgin olive oil, mix well, and season to perfection.

6 Mix the remaining gochujang into the yogurt and divide between the buns. Halve the chicken pieces and pile up on the bun bottoms along with the slaw, put the bun tops on, press together and enjoy! Serve any extra slaw on the side.

ENERGY	FAT	SAT FAT	PROTEIN	CARBS	SUGARS	SALT	FIBER
665kcal	22g	5g	33.6g	83.7g	20.3g	2.6g	8.5g

Hoisin duck cups

 Serves 2   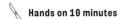 Hands on 10 minutes   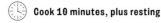 Cook 10 minutes, plus resting   1 Drawer

2 x 5-oz duck breast
fillets, skin on

2 plums

1 nest of vermicelli rice
noodles (about 1½ oz)

1 little gem lettuce

12 oz crunchy veg, such as
carrots, radishes, cucumbers,
zucchini and snow peas

½ a fresh red chili

1 lime

2 tbsp hoisin sauce

2 tbsp crunchy peanut
& sesame chili oil
or salsa macha

1 Pat the duck dry with paper towels, then score the skin in a crosshatch fashion at ½-inch intervals. Rub with 1 tablespoon of olive oil, a small pinch of sea salt and a generous sprinkling of black pepper. Halve and pit the plums.

2 Use a heatproof ramekin or two metal cookie cutters to raise the air-fryer shelf up (meaning you'll get crispy duck skin). Lay in a sheet of parchment paper, then place the duck on top, skin-side up, with the plum halves around it, cut-side down. Cook for 10 minutes at 400°F, or until the duck is crispy on the outside but still pink in the middle. Remove and let rest for 5 minutes, then pinch off and discard the plum skins.

3 In a bowl, cover the noodles with boiling water and let sit to rehydrate, then drain. Separate out the lettuce leaves. Prep and coarsely grate the crunchy veg, finely grate the chili and lime zest, then toss it all with the lime juice and a pinch of salt. Put the hoisin sauce and chili oil into little dipping bowls.

4 Thinly slice the duck breasts, then serve it all together on a big board and tuck in, having fun loading your lettuce cups with all the delicious things.

ENERGY	FAT	SAT FAT	PROTEIN	CARBS	SUGARS	SALT	FIBER
603kcal	26.9g	5.4g	47.3g	43g	18.7g	1.6g	6.4g

Smoky pepper fish pie

 Serves 2    Hands on 13 minutes   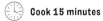 Cook 15 minutes   2 Drawer

1 sheet of puff pastry
(about 7 x 9 inches)

1 egg

2 tbsp couscous

2 long, thin frozen
white fish fillets

12 oz asparagus

8 oz baby spinach

1 clove of garlic

1 large jarred roasted
red pepper (about 2½ oz)

1 tsp smoked paprika

½ cup sliced almonds,
plus extra for sprinkling

½ a lemon

1 Preheat the large air-fryer drawer for 2 minutes to 400°F. Unroll the pastry, leaving it on its paper. Beat the egg and brush over the whole surface, then sprinkle with the couscous, leaving a ¾-inch border around the edge. Place the frozen fish fillets on top ½ inch apart, then twist and fold in the exposed pastry to make a crust. Eggwash the crust, then carefully use the paper to help you lift the whole thing into the large drawer and cook for 10 minutes.

2 Snap the woody ends off the asparagus, rub the spears with ½ tablespoon of olive oil, season with sea salt and black pepper, then place in the small drawer and cook for 8 minutes at 350°F, adding the spinach to wilt for the last couple of minutes.

3 Pour the remaining eggwash into a blender, then peel and add the garlic along with the red pepper, paprika, almonds, ½ tablespoon of oil and a pinch each of salt and pepper. Blitz until smooth.

4 Open the large drawer and pour the smoky sauce over and around the fish, keeping it inside the pastry crust. Sprinkle with a few extra almonds, then gently shut the drawer. Cook for a final 5 minutes at 400°F, or until the sauce has set. Serve with the green veg and lemon wedges on the side.

ENERGY	FAT	SAT FAT	PROTEIN	CARBS	SUGARS	SALT	FIBER
790kcal	43.8g	12.6g	50.9g	66.8g	6.9g	1.6g	9.8g

Roast chicken dinner for one

 Serves 1  Hands on 10 minutes  Cook 42 minutes   2 Drawer

6 oz Yukon Gold potatoes

6 oz rutabaga or turnip

2 cloves of garlic

2 sprigs of thyme

1 lemon

1 chicken leg (about 8 oz)

3 tbsp all-purpose flour

1 medium egg

2 tbsp reduced-fat milk

4 oz baby spinach

1 Scrub the potatoes, peel the rutabaga and slice both ¼ inch thick, then place in the large air-fryer drawer with the whole unpeeled garlic cloves. Add the thyme, finely grate in the lemon zest, then toss it all with 2 tablespoons of olive oil and a pinch each of sea salt and black pepper. Shake into an even layer, tucking the garlic underneath the veg.

2 Season the chicken leg and place it on top of the veg, skin-side down. Cook it all for 40 minutes at 375°F, or until golden and cooked through, flipping the chicken halfway and tossing the veg at the same time.

3 To make the Yorkshire pudding, beat the flour, egg, milk, 2 teaspoons of water and a pinch of salt together until smooth. With 20 minutes to go, remove the shelf from the small drawer, add 1 tablespoon of oil and heat for 5 minutes at 400°F. Gently pull out the drawer, pour in the batter, and cook for 15 minutes, or until puffed up and golden.

4 Transfer the chicken, potatoes, rutabaga and garlic to a plate. Carefully remove the air-fryer shelf, then squeeze the soft garlic into the drawer, discarding the skins, add the spinach, squeeze in the lemon juice and season. Toss the leaves to coat them in the residual cooking juices and cook for 2 minutes at 400°F, or until wilted.

5 Season the spinach to perfection and pile alongside the chicken and veg with the Yorkshire pudding. Great served with gravy and your favorite mustard.

ENERGY	FAT	SAT FAT	PROTEIN	CARBS	SUGARS	SALT	FIBER
918kcal	52.5g	10.7g	44.7g	72.3g	13.2g	2.2g	9g

Falafel burgers

 Serves 2    Hands on 14 minutes    Cook 15 minutes   1 Drawer

1 x 15-oz can of chickpeas

2 carrots

2 scallions

½ a bunch of Italian parsley (about ½ oz)

2 heaping tbsp chickpea flour

2½ tsp baharat spice mix

2 tbsp toasted sesame seeds

2 burger buns

1 small clove of garlic

2 generous tbsp plain yogurt

1 Drain the chickpeas and add to a food processor. Wash, chop and add 1 carrot, trim and add the scallions, then tear in the parsley stems, reserving the leaves. Add the chickpea flour and 2 teaspoons of baharat, along with a good pinch each of sea salt and black pepper, and blitz until combined.

2 Divide the mixture in half and shape into ¾-inch-thick patties. Put the sesame seeds on a plate, then spend a bit of time patting them onto the burgers, helping them to stick. Cook in the air-fryer drawer for 15 minutes at 350°F, or until the burgers are crisp, adding the buns cut-side up for the last minute.

3 Wash the remaining carrot, then shave into ribbons. Toss with the parsley leaves and ½ tablespoon each of red wine vinegar and extra virgin olive oil, then season to perfection.

4 Finely grate the garlic into a small bowl, stir in the yogurt and remaining ½ teaspoon of baharat, and season to perfection, then spread inside the buns. Place the falafel burgers on the bun bottoms, top with the carrot and parsley salad, put the bun tops on and devour.

Vegan love

Choose vegan buns and simply swap in a vegan yogurt.

ENERGY	FAT	SAT FAT	PROTEIN	CARBS	SUGARS	SALT	FIBER
590kcal	16.8g	3.7g	17.6g	84.4g	10.7g	1.7g	10.9g

Prosciutto baked fish & garlicky beans

 Serves 2    Hands on 7 minutes    Cook 17 minutes   2 Drawer

2 cloves of garlic

4 sprigs of rosemary

3 tbsp blanched almonds

⅓ cup sun-dried tomatoes in oil

1 oz Parmesan cheese

2 x 5-oz skinless white fish fillets, pin-boned

4 slices of prosciutto or Parma ham

½ a lemon

1 x 15-oz can of white beans

6 oz baby spinach

1 Peel and thinly slice the garlic, pick and finely chop 2 sprigs of rosemary, then remove the shelf from the small air-fryer drawer and scatter it all into the base. Drizzle in 1 tablespoon of olive oil, then cook for 5 minutes at 400°F, or until the garlic is lightly golden.

2 Meanwhile, bash the almonds and sun-dried tomatoes in a mortar and pestle with ½ tablespoon of oil from the tomato jar and a few gratings of Parmesan until you have a thick paste, then spoon over the fish. Drape 2 slices of prosciutto over each fillet, also tucking in a rosemary sprig. Drizzle with ½ tablespoon of oil from the tomato jar and place in the large drawer, then cut the lemon half into wedges and place alongside. Cook for 10 minutes at 400°F, or until cooked through.

3 Stir the beans and half their juice into the small drawer with 1 tablespoon of red wine vinegar and cook for 10 minutes at 400°F, or until piping hot, then season to perfection with sea salt and black pepper, and divide between plates.

4 Place the fish on top of the beans. Pack the spinach into the large drawer, season, and cook for 2 minutes at 400°F, or until just wilted, then drizzle with a little extra virgin olive oil and serve alongside the fish. Finely grate on the remaining Parmesan and serve with the jammy lemon wedges.

ENERGY	FAT	SAT FAT	PROTEIN	CARBS	SUGARS	SALT	FIBER
563kcal	29.4g	5.9g	52.8g	22.6g	2.8g	1.8g	9.9g

BBQ chicken lollipops

 Serves 2   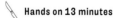 **Hands on 13 minutes**    **Cook 33 minutes**   **2 Drawer**

6 chicken drumsticks

1 tsp Chinese
five spice powder

2 heaping tbsp
panko breadcrumbs

2 heaping tbsp sesame seeds

1 English cucumber

4 scallions

2 oranges

1 tbsp crunchy peanut
& sesame chili oil
or salsa macha

2 tbsp BBQ or hoisin sauce

1 You can cook the drumsticks as they are, or follow my lollipop-style hack – it takes a few minutes but makes for great eating! Simply use a small sharp knife to slice around the bone end of a drumstick and, holding it by the bone end, scrape the meat down toward the fat end, then use your hand to push it down so it almost folds in on itself, and repeat.

2 Toss the chicken with the five spice, a pinch each of sea salt and black pepper, and 1 tablespoon of olive oil, then evenly space in the large air-fryer drawer and cook for 30 minutes at 375°F, or until cooked through.

3 With 15 minutes to go, remove the shelf from the small drawer. Tip in the bread-crumbs and sesame seeds and cook for 15 minutes at 375°F, or until lightly golden, shaking the drawer twice. Spread onto a serving plate once done.

4 Quarter the cucumber lengthwise, remove the seedy core and chop into chunks, trim and thinly slice the scallions, peel 1½ oranges, slice into rounds, then place it all in a bowl. Add the chili oil, squeeze in the remaining orange juice to make a dressing, toss together and season to perfection.

5 Remove the chicken lollipops and coat in the BBQ sauce, then return to the large drawer and cook for just 3 minutes at 300°F. Dunk the chicken lollipops in the sesame crumb and serve with the salad.

ENERGY	FAT	SAT FAT	PROTEIN	CARBS	SUGARS	SALT	FIBER
572kcal	29g	5.7g	45.4g	36.2g	13.8g	1.4g	2.1g

Cauliflower cheese pasta

 Serves 4    **Hands on 10 minutes**    **Cook 35 minutes**   **1 Drawer**

1 lb frozen cauliflower florets

1⅔ cups reduced-fat milk

1 tbsp English or Dijon mustard

12 oz penne pasta

4 oz Cheddar cheese

1 x 3-inch piece of fresh
garlic bread (about 3½ oz)

1 Remove the shelf from the air-fryer drawer, then add the cauliflower, milk and mustard. Give it a stir, then cook for 25 minutes at 400°F, or until the cauliflower is soft. A skin will form on the sauce, but don't worry, it will taste delicious and we'll blitz it all up later anyway.

2 Meanwhile, cook the pasta in a large pot of boiling salted water for 2 minutes less than the package instructions – we want it to still have a slight bite at this point – then drain, reserving a generous cupful of starchy cooking water.

3 Coarsely grate most of the cheese over the cauliflower, tear in one-quarter of the garlic bread, then use an immersion blender to carefully blitz the contents of the drawer until really smooth and silky. Stir in the pasta, season to perfection with sea salt and black pepper, and loosen with splashes of reserved cooking water until you have a creamy consistency.

4 Finely chop the remaining garlic bread, then sprinkle over the pasta. Grate on the remaining cheese and cook for a final 10 minutes at 400°F, or until golden and bubbling. Delicious served with lemony-dressed arugula.

ENERGY	FAT	SAT FAT	PROTEIN	CARBS	SUGARS	SALT	FIBER
444kcal	18g	9.1g	23g	77.2g	10g	1.6g	2.4g

Fragrant chicken in a bag

 Serves 1 + 3 freezer paste portions   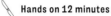 Hands on 12 minutes   Cook 25 minutes   1 Drawer

1 nest of vermicelli rice noodles (about 1½ oz)

12 lime leaves

3-inch piece of ginger

2 cloves of garlic

1 stalk of lemongrass

1½ fresh red chilies

1 bunch of cilantro (about 1 oz)

¼ cup reduced-sodium soy sauce

toasted sesame oil

1 x 5-oz boneless, skinless chicken breast

1 baby bok choy

3 oz (about 1¼ cups) sugar snap peas

3 oz fresh baby corn (about ¾ cup)

2 scallions

1 tbsp unsalted roasted peanuts

½ a lime

1   In a bowl, cover the noodles with boiling water and let sit to soften for a few minutes, then drain and refresh under cold running water.

2   Tear the lime leaves into a mini food processor, discarding any tough stalks. Peel, roughly chop and add the ginger and garlic, chop and add the lemongrass and 1 chili, most of the cilantro, stems and all, reserving a few nice leaves, and a pinch of sea salt. Add the soy and 1 teaspoon of sesame oil and blitz into a paste. Divide the paste into four, keeping 1 portion for now and freezing the rest for future meals.

3   Score deeply into the chicken a few times at an angle and rub with half the paste portion. Halve the bok choy, sugar snaps and baby corn, trim and thinly slice the scallions, then toss it all with the remaining paste half-portion.

4   Tear off a large sheet of heavy-duty aluminum foil (about 24 inches long), fold it in half, then open it up like a book and rub one side with sesame oil. Top with the noodles and veg. Thinly slice and sprinkle on the remaining chili, then place the chicken on top. Fold over the foil to create a parcel, twisting the edges to seal, and adding 3 tablespoons of water before sealing the final side. Place in the air-fryer drawer and cook for 25 minutes at 400°F, or until the chicken is cooked through.

5   Remove the bag to a serving plate and carefully tear open the foil. Crush over the nuts, sprinkle with the cilantro leaves and finish with a squeeze of lime.

ENERGY	FAT	SAT FAT	PROTEIN	CARBS	SUGARS	SALT	FIBER
655kcal	20g	3.6g	52.9g	64.4g	9.5g	1.8g	4.1g

Celebrating all the wonderful ways you can hero humble veggies in the air fryer

Big up the veg

Tomato & mozzarella tart

 Serves 2    Hands on 15 minutes    Cook 30 minutes   1 Drawer

1 lb ripe tomatoes

1 sheet of puff pastry
(about 7 x 9 inches)

6 kalamata olives, with pits

½ a fresh red chili

½ x 4-oz ball of mozzarella

2 sprigs of basil

1 Halve the tomatoes, then use your fingers to scrape out the seeds. Remove the shelf from the air-fryer drawer and add the tomato halves, 1 tablespoon of olive oil and a pinch each of sea salt and black pepper. Toss together, arrange the tomatoes cut-side down, and cook for 15 minutes at 400°F, or until soft and golden.

2 Gently stretch or roll out the pastry to the size of the drawer. Lay the pastry on top of the tomatoes, carefully poking and tucking it in at the edges. Cook for 15 minutes at 400°F, or until dark golden and puffed up.

3 Meanwhile, smash, pit and tear up the olives and thinly slice the chili. Dress with 1 tablespoon of red wine vinegar and ½ tablespoon of extra virgin olive oil, then season to perfection.

4 Carefully and confidently flip the tart out of the drawer onto a board, tear on the mozzarella and basil leaves, spoon on the olive mixture and serve. Nice with a simple arugula salad on the side.

ENERGY	FAT	SAT FAT	PROTEIN	CARBS	SUGARS	SALT	FIBER
302kcal	21g	9.9g	8.5g	19.9g	4.2g	1.3g	1.6g

Broccoli soup & cheesy soldiers

 Serves 2    Hands on 8 minutes    Cook 20 minutes   2 Drawer

1 lb frozen broccoli florets

4 scallions

3 tbsp mixed seeds, such as sunflower, pumpkin, sesame and poppy

1 large slice of bread

3 oz Cheddar cheese

1⅔ cups hot vegetable stock

1 bunch of Italian parsley (about 1 oz)

1 Remove the shelf from the large air-fryer drawer, add the broccoli, then trim, roughly chop and add the scallions, drizzle with 1 tablespoon of olive oil, season with sea salt and black pepper and toss well. Cook for 15 minutes at 400°F, or until the broccoli is soft, shaking the drawer occasionally.

2 Use your fingertips to press the seeds into the surface of the bread, drizzle with 1 teaspoon of oil and grate on a layer of cheese. Cook in the small drawer for 7 minutes at 350°F, or until golden and crisp, then slice.

3 Once the broccoli is soft, remove the drawer from the air fryer, grate in the remaining cheese, pour in the veg stock and tear in most of the bunch of parsley, stems and all.

4 Carefully blitz with an immersion blender until smooth, adding a splash of water, if needed. Season to perfection, then gently return the drawer and cook for 5 minutes at 350°F, or until piping hot.

5 Divide between mugs or bowls, pick over the remaining parsley, and drizzle with a little extra virgin olive oil, if you like. Serve with the seeded toast soldiers.

ENERGY	FAT	SAT FAT	PROTEIN	CARBS	SUGARS	SALT	FIBER
487kcal	27.9g	10.9g	25.9g	33.4g	6.4g	1.8g	9.1g

Sicilian eggplant pasta

 Serves 2   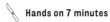 Hands on 7 minutes    Cook 30 minutes   1 Drawer

2 small eggplants
(about 8 oz each)

2 cloves of garlic

8 green olives, with pits

½ a bunch of basil (about ½ oz)

1 tbsp drained capers

2 tbsp pine nuts

1 x 14-oz can of
whole tomatoes

6 oz dried pasta

1 oz Parmesan cheese

1 Remove the shelf from the air-fryer drawer. Chop the eggplants into generous 1-inch chunks, place in the drawer and toss with a pinch each of sea salt and black pepper, then cook for 15 minutes at 400°F, or until starting to soften, shaking halfway.

2 Peel and slice the garlic. Smash, pit and tear up the olives. Finely chop the basil stems, reserving the leaves. When the time's up, add it all to the drawer along with the capers, pine nuts and 1 tablespoon of olive oil. Toss well and cook for 5 minutes at 400°F.

3 Pour in the tomatoes, crushing them through your fingers, then fill the can halfway with water, give it a swirl, and pour into the drawer. Cook for a final 10 minutes at 400°F, or until reduced and saucy, then tear in most of the basil leaves, saving the baby ones for garnish, add a splash of red wine vinegar and season to perfection.

4 Meanwhile, cook the pasta in a pot of boiling salted water according to the package instructions, then drain, reserving a generous cupful of starchy cooking water.

5 Tip the drained pasta into the drawer and toss well, loosening with a little reserved cooking water, if needed. Divide between bowls, finely grate on the Parmesan, sprinkle with the reserved baby basil leaves and serve.

ENERGY	FAT	SAT FAT	PROTEIN	CARBS	SUGARS	SALT	FIBER
493kcal	13.2g	3.5g	17.9g	82.7g	17.3g	1.4g	12.6g

Sweet potato & black bean tacos

 Serves 2    Hands on 12 minutes    Cook 30 minutes   1 Drawer

2 scallions

1 x 15-oz can of black beans

2 tsp Cajun seasoning

2 sweet potatoes
(about 8 oz each)

4 regular flour tortillas

6 oz peeled watermelon

½ a bunch of cilantro
(about ½ oz)

½ a fresh red chili

1 lime

1 oz feta cheese

1 Trim and thinly slice the scallions, then remove the shelf from the air-fryer drawer and scatter them into the base. Add the beans, along with half their juice, stir in half the Cajun seasoning, then replace the shelf.

2 Scrub the sweet potatoes, then chop into generous 1-inch chunks and add to the drawer. Drizzle with 1 tablespoon each of red wine vinegar and olive oil, add the remaining Cajun seasoning and a pinch each of sea salt and black pepper, and rub together. Cook for 30 minutes at 350°F, or until soft and golden, shaking halfway, and adding the tortillas to warm through for the last 2 minutes.

3 Meanwhile, finely dice the watermelon, finely chop the cilantro stems, reserving the leaves, seed and finely chop the chili, then squeeze on half the lime juice, add ½ tablespoon of extra virgin olive oil, gently toss together, and season to perfection.

4 Remove the tortillas and sweet potato chunks and carefully remove the shelf. Roughly chop the cilantro leaves and add most of them to the beans, reserving a few for garnish. Roughly mash the beans to create a thick saucy consistency, season to perfection, then spoon onto the tortillas.

5 Top with the sweet potato chunks and watermelon salsa, crumble on the feta, and sprinkle with the reserved cilantro leaves. Serve with lime wedges.

ENERGY	FAT	SAT FAT	PROTEIN	CARBS	SUGARS	SALT	FIBER
614kcal	10.9g	3.3g	21.6g	102.5g	21.4g	1.8g	20.3g

Lemon & chili broccolini

 Serves 2    Hands on 5 minutes   Cook 7 minutes   1 Drawer

Remove the shelf from the air-fryer drawer. Trim **8 oz of broccolini**, halving any thicker stalks lengthwise, place in the drawer and toss with 1 teaspoon of olive oil. Cook for 7 minutes at 350°F, or until softened and starting to char. Meanwhile, peel and finely grate **½ a clove of garlic** into a large bowl, add 1 tablespoon of extra virgin olive oil, then finely grate in the zest of **1 lemon** and squeeze in half the juice. Tip in the cooked broccolini, toss to coat, season to perfection with sea salt and black pepper, and finish with a pinch of **dried red chili flakes**. Delicious served with steamed fish or mozzarella.

ENERGY	FAT	SAT FAT	PROTEIN	CARBS	SUGARS	SALT	FIBER
103kcal	8.1g	1.2g	4.5g	3.5g	2.1g	0.1g	4.4g

Creamy mustard cabbage

 Serves 2   Hands on 3 minutes   Cook 12 minutes   1 Drawer

Remove the shelf from the air-fryer drawer. Thinly slice **1 small head of Savoy cabbage (about 1 lb)** and pack into the drawer. Massage with **1 generous tablespoon each of grainy mustard** and olive oil and **2 tablespoons of cream cheese**, then cook for 12 minutes at 350°F, or until the cabbage is soft and beginning to get dark and gnarly, shaking halfway. Season to perfection with sea salt and black pepper, and serve. Lovely alongside golden chicken or a pork chop.

ENERGY	FAT	SAT FAT	PROTEIN	CARBS	SUGARS	SALT	FIBER
195kcal	14.2g	5.4g	7.1g	9.8g	9.8g	0.6g	8.2g

Spiced squash rice

 Serves 4    Hands on 10 minutes    Cook 50 minutes   1 Drawer

½ a butternut squash (about 1¼ lb)

2 heaping tbsp of your favorite curry paste

2 fresh red chilies

1 x 15-oz can of chickpeas

1 x 8½-oz package of cooked basmati rice

2 tbsp unsweetened shredded coconut

2 eggs

4 oz paneer or halloumi cheese

4 scallions

8 oz baby spinach

2 sprigs of cilantro

1 Carefully slice the squash into ¼-inch-thick slices (peel first, if you like), seeding if necessary, then place in the air-fryer drawer and toss with half the curry paste and 1 tablespoon of olive oil. Prick and add the whole chilies and cook for 30 minutes at 350°F, shaking halfway.

2 Drain the chickpeas and tip into a large bowl along with the rice, coconut and the remaining curry paste. Crack in the eggs, and cube up and add the paneer. Trim, thinly slice and mix in most of the scallions, saving a few for garnish.

3 When the time's up, tip the squash into the bowl, then slice and add the chilies (seed, if you like). Mash a few bits of the squash and mix it all together.

4 Carefully remove the shelf from the drawer and tip the rice mixture back in. Cook for 20 minutes at 350°F, stirring halfway to mix the nice dark gnarly bits back through, and adding the spinach to wilt for the last 5 minutes.

5 Give it one last stir, season to perfection with sea salt and black pepper, then plate up, sprinkle with the reserved scallions, pick over the cilantro leaves, and dig in! Great with a bit of yogurt, mango chutney and a couple of pappadams on the side.

ENERGY	FAT	SAT FAT	PROTEIN	CARBS	SUGARS	SALT	FIBER
413kcal	19.1g	7.5g	19.4g	43g	10.5g	1.1g	6.6g

Sticky eggplant noodles

 Serves 1   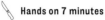 Hands on 7 minutes   Cook 20 minutes   1 Drawer

1 small eggplant (about 8 oz)

1 clove of garlic

1 baby bok choy

1 tbsp unsalted roasted peanuts

1 tbsp sweet red chili sauce

6 oz fresh thick udon noodles (or cooked, drained udon noodles)

4 scallions

½ a fresh red chili

½ a little gem lettuce

2 sprigs of mint or cilantro

1 tbsp crunchy peanut & sesame chili oil or salsa macha

1 tbsp balsamic vinegar

1 Slice the eggplant lengthwise ½ inch thick, then into long ½-inch-wide strips. Remove the air-fryer shelf, scatter the eggplant into the drawer and cook for 15 minutes at 400°F, shaking halfway.

2 Peel and thinly slice the garlic. Quarter the bok choy lengthwise. When the time's up, pull out the drawer, scatter in the garlic and peanuts, spoon on the sweet chili sauce, then shake to coat. Add the bok choy alongside and cook for 5 minutes at 400°F, or until the eggplant is soft and sticky.

3 In a bowl, cover the noodles with boiling water to soften and set aside. Trim the scallions and thinly slice with the chili. Separate out the lettuce leaves. Pick the herb leaves.

4 Drain the noodles and add to the drawer with most of the chili and scallions, the chili oil and balsamic. Toss together well, season to perfection with sea salt and black pepper, then transfer to a serving bowl. Add the lettuce leaves on the side, sprinkle with the remaining chili and scallions, along with the herb leaves, then serve.

ENERGY	FAT	SAT FAT	PROTEIN	CARBS	SUGARS	SALT	FIBER
489kcal	13.7g	1.8g	16.4g	75g	24.2g	1.3g	12.2g

Sage & bacon sprouts

 Serves 2   Hands on 5 minutes   Cook 10 minutes   1 Drawer

Trim and halve **8 oz of Brussels sprouts**, place them in the air-fryer drawer and toss with 2 tablespoons of olive oil, a pinch of sea salt and the leaves from **2 sprigs of sage**. Lay **4 slices of bacon** on top or crumble on **1 handful of vacuum-packed chestnuts** and cook for 10 minutes at 350°F, or until the bacon is crisp and the sprouts are soft. Finish with a drizzle of **runny honey**, to taste. Perfect for a festive spread.

ENERGY	FAT	SAT FAT	PROTEIN	CARBS	SUGARS	SALT	FIBER
251kcal	19.4g	4.1g	6.9g	14.7g	3.2g	1.3g	3.8g

Harissa green beans

 Serves 2    Hands on 3 minutes   Cook 10 minutes   1 Drawer

Trim **8 oz of green beans**, place in the air-fryer drawer and toss with 1 table-spoon each of red wine vinegar and olive oil, **1 teaspoon of harissa paste**, a pinch each of sea salt and black pepper, and **3 tablespoons of blanched hazelnuts**. Cook for 10 minutes at 350°F, or until the beans are soft and starting to char. On a serving plate, ripple **1 teaspoon of harissa paste** through **2 tablespoons of Greek yogurt**, then pile the green beans and hazelnuts on top, drizzling with any nice juices from the drawer. Great as it is, as part of a salad spread or with seared steak.

ENERGY	FAT	SAT FAT	PROTEIN	CARBS	SUGARS	SALT	FIBER
164kcal	14.7g	2.4g	5.8g	4.8g	3.6g	0.6g	4.7g

Sticky onion tart

 Serves 2    Hands on 9 minutes    Cook 35 minutes   1 Drawer

4 small red onions

4 sprigs of thyme

2 tbsp good
orange marmalade

1½ tbsp unsalted butter

1 sheet of puff pastry
(about 7 x 9 inches)

¼ cup walnut halves

2 oz fresh goat cheese (chèvre)

1 Remove the shelf from the air-fryer drawer. Peel the onions, slice into rounds just under ½ inch thick, and put in the drawer with the thyme. Loosen the marmalade with 2 tablespoons of water, pour over the top and toss to coat, then arrange the onions in an even layer. Dot on the butter and cook for 25 minutes at 400°F, or until soft and sticky, shaking halfway.

2 Gently stretch or roll out the pastry to the size of the drawer. Lay the pastry on top of the onions, carefully poking and tucking it in at the edges. Cook for 10 minutes at 400°F, or until dark golden and puffed up.

3 Carefully and confidently flip the tart out of the drawer onto a board, crumble on the walnuts and dot with the goat cheese. Delicious served with a simple green salad and a mustardy dressing.

ENERGY	FAT	SAT FAT	PROTEIN	CARBS	SUGARS	SALT	FIBER
690kcal	41.4g	20g	13.1g	67.9g	32.5g	0.6g	5.7g

Tomato tortilla soup

 Serves 2    Hands on 7 minutes    Cook 37 minutes   1 Drawer

2 red bell peppers

12 oz ripe tomatoes

1 onion

1 tsp ground cinnamon

1 heaping tsp dried oregano

½ a bunch of cilantro (about ½ oz)

1 tbsp jarred sliced jalapeños

1 regular flour tortilla

2 oz Cheddar cheese

½ a lime

1 Seed and roughly chop the peppers. Halve the tomatoes. Peel the onion and slice into ½-inch-thick rounds. Remove the shelf from the air-fryer drawer, place all the veg inside, and toss with the cinnamon, oregano, ½ tablespoon of olive oil and a pinch each of sea salt and black pepper. Cook for 30 minutes at 400°F, or until soft, shaking halfway.

2 Remove the drawer and add most of the cilantro, stems and all, 1 tablespoon of brine from the jalapeño jar, and 1⅔ cups of boiling water. Use an immersion blender to blitz the soup to your liking, then season to perfection.

3 Tear in the tortilla, grate on the cheese, add the jalapeños, then return the drawer to the air fryer and cook for 7 minutes at 400°F, or until golden.

4 Divide the soup between bowls, top with the remaining cilantro leaves, serve with lime wedges, and slurp away!

ENERGY	FAT	SAT FAT	PROTEIN	CARBS	SUGARS	SALT	FIBER
295kcal	13.4g	6g	12g	32.6g	14.9g	1.5g	6.3g

Crazy for kale chips

Crisping things up is what air fryers are known for, making them the perfect choice for a batch of kale chips. Whether you choose to go neutral with good old sea salt, or to add a bit of spice, is up to you.

 Hands on 2 minutes   **Cook 10 minutes**   **1 Drawer**

Remove the shelf from the air-fryer drawer. Remove and discard any large stems from **6 oz of kale**, tear into bite-size pieces, then load it into the drawer and massage with a generous pinch of sea salt and 2 tablespoons of olive oil, until the leaves darken and soften slightly. Cook for 10 minutes at 350°F, or until crispy, shaking every couple of minutes. Delicious just as it is, or you can try seasoning with a little smoked paprika or cayenne pepper for a bit of a kick, or any of your favorite spice blends.

Squashage rolls

½ a butternut squash
(about 1¼ lb)

2 tbsp dukkah

1 pinch of dried red chili flakes

1 x 8½-oz package of cooked
mixed grains

4 oz feta cheese

1 large egg

1 sheet of puff pastry
(about 9 x 14 inches)

1 Cut the squash into generous 1-inch chunks (peel first, if you like), seeding if necessary, toss with 1 tablespoon each of dukkah and olive oil, the chili flakes and a pinch each of sea salt and black pepper. Place in the air-fryer drawer and cook for 30 minutes at 350°F, or until soft and caramelized, shaking halfway.

2 Transfer the squash to a large bowl and let cool, then mash it up with a fork or potato masher. Crumble in the grains and feta. Beat the egg in a small bowl, then pour three-quarters into the squash mixture, season, and mix well.

3 Unroll the pastry sheet on its paper. Pile the filling lengthwise down the middle, slightly off-center, shaping it into a nice, thick sausage shape. Lightly brush one of the long sides with some of the reserved eggwash, then use the paper to help you fold the pastry over the filling, pressing down to secure and sealing with a fork. Brush all over with the remaining eggwash, then score lightly at ¾-inch intervals. Sprinkle with the remaining dukkah.

4 Preheat the air fryer for 2 minutes to 400°F. Cut the squashage roll into 4 equal pieces on the paper, trimming any excess paper. Cook 2 at a time for 20 minutes at 400°F, or until golden and puffed up. Delicious with piccalilli or pickle relish and a zingy fresh salad on the side, or as part of a bigger spread.

ENERGY	FAT	SAT FAT	PROTEIN	CARBS	SUGARS	SALT	FIBER
606kcal	34g	14.6g	17.4g	72.4g	8.4g	2g	7.3g

Stuffed mushrooms

 Serves 2  Hands on 12 minutes 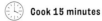 Cook 15 minutes   1 Drawer

4 portobello mushrooms

1 x 14½-oz can of peeled new potatoes (or 10 oz of peeled, cooked potatoes)

2 oz Taleggio cheese

½ a bunch of rosemary (about ⅓ oz)

1 lemon

2 slices of sourdough bread (about 3½ oz total)

1 little gem lettuce

1 endive

2 handfuls of arugula

1 To make the stuffing, remove and finely chop the mushroom stems, then place in a bowl. Drain and add the potatoes, then tear in the cheese in small pieces. Pick, finely chop and add most of the rosemary, finely grate in half the lemon zest, add a good pinch each of sea salt and black pepper and mash well. Evenly divide the mixture between the mushroom caps, packing it in nicely.

2 In a food processor, blitz the bread into crumbs with the remaining rosemary and 1 tablespoon of olive oil, then sprinkle over the mushrooms.

3 Evenly space in the air-fryer drawer and cook for 15 minutes at 350°F, or until the crumbs are golden and the mushrooms are soft.

4 Meanwhile, cut the little gem into thin wedges, trim and thinly slice the endive core and separate out the leaves, toss with the arugula, a good squeeze of lemon juice and ½ tablespoon of extra virgin olive oil, then season to perfection. Serve alongside the stuffed mushrooms.

ENERGY	FAT	SAT FAT	PROTEIN	CARBS	SUGARS	SALT	FIBER
389kcal	17.8g	6g	15.1g	42.3g	4g	1.8g	3.6g

Gochujang cabbage

 Serves 2   Hands on 3 minutes   Cook 16 minutes   1 Drawer

Pour 2 tablespoons of water into the air-fryer drawer. Cut **1 small conehead or napa cabbage** lengthwise into 6 wedges, then, in a bowl, rub with ½ tablespoon of olive oil and 1 tablespoon of red wine vinegar, a pinch of black pepper and then **1 tablespoon of gochujang paste**. Evenly space in the drawer, cut-side down, cook for 10 minutes at 325°F, or until softening, then flip and cook for another 6 minutes at 350°F, or until starting to char. Sprinkle with some **mixed toasted seeds**, and serve. Nice with noodles, tofu or chicken.

ENERGY	FAT	SAT FAT	PROTEIN	CARBS	SUGARS	SALT	FIBER
128kcal	3.9g	0.6g	7.6g	16g	14.1g	0.6g	12.8g

Dukkah spinach

Serves 2   Hands on 2 minutes   Cook 4 minutes   1 Drawer

Remove the shelf from the air-fryer drawer and pack in **8 oz of baby spinach**. Evenly sprinkle with **1 tablespoon of dukkah** and the finely grated zest of **½ a lemon**, then cook for 4 minutes at 350°F, or until the spinach has wilted, stirring halfway. Season to perfection with sea salt, black pepper and a squeeze of lemon juice, and finish with a drizzle of extra virgin olive oil. Brilliant with roasted veg, such as squash or cauliflower, or with golden chicken.

ENERGY	FAT	SAT FAT	PROTEIN	CARBS	SUGARS	SALT	FIBER
67kcal	4.6g	0.6g	4.2g	1.7g	0.1g	0.2g	2.9g

Scruffy squash lasagna

½ a butternut squash
(about 1¼ lb)

1 good pinch of
ground cinnamon

1 pinch of dried red chili flakes

1⅓ cups cottage cheese

3 eggs

1 bunch of basil (about 1 oz)

2 oz Parmesan cheese

8 oz fresh lasagna sheets

2 tsp basil pesto

1 Cut the squash into ¾-inch chunks (peel first, if you like), seeding if necessary. Place in the air-fryer drawer and toss with the cinnamon, chili flakes, 1 tablespoon of olive oil and a pinch each of sea salt and black pepper. Cook for 30 minutes at 350°F, or until soft and caramelized.

2 Put the cottage cheese into a large bowl, crack in the eggs, pick, chop and add the basil leaves, grate in half the Parmesan, season, mix together, then tear in the lasagna sheets. Add the soft squash, roughly mashing it with a fork, then mix in ⅔ cup of water.

3 Carefully line the shelf and the sides of the drawer with scrunched-up damp parchment paper, keeping the paper away from the heating element, then evenly pack in the mixture. Cook for 15 minutes at 350°F.

4 Pull out the drawer, mix well, smooth it down, finely grate on the remaining Parmesan, drizzle with a little oil and cook for a final 15 minutes at 350°F, or until golden and cooked through. Let rest in the drawer for a few minutes.

5 Use the parchment paper to help you lift the lasagna out, dollop with the pesto, slice and serve. Great with an arugula and Parmesan salad.

Tip: If you can't find fresh lasagna sheets, substitute dried lasagna noodles that have been cooked to al dente, drained and patted dry.

ENERGY	FAT	SAT FAT	PROTEIN	CARBS	SUGARS	SALT	FIBER
530kcal	24.5g	9.8g	29.8g	48.5g	13.9g	1.6g	5.6g

Med veg & epic tomato dressing

 Serves 2   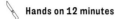 Hands on 12 minutes    Cook 40 minutes   2 Drawer

2 small red onions

1 lemon

1 bulb of garlic

1 small eggplant (about 8 oz)

1 zucchini

1 large ripe tomato

1 pinch of dried red chili flakes

6 kalamata olives, with pits

½ cup plain yogurt

3 sprigs of mint

3 sprigs of Italian parsley

1 oz feta cheese

1 Peel the onions, then halve with the lemon. Remove the shelf from the small air-fryer drawer, place the onions and lemon inside with the whole unpeeled garlic bulb and cook for 40 minutes at 400°F, or until soft and delicious, removing the lemon halves after 15 minutes.

2 Halve the eggplant and zucchini lengthwise, score the skin side of each in a crosshatch pattern at ¼-inch intervals, then place flesh-side down in the large drawer and cook for 30 minutes at 400°F, or until golden.

3 For the dressing, put 2 tablespoons of extra virgin olive oil into a shallow bowl. Use tongs to squeeze in the juice from one jammy lemon half. Halve the tomato and finely grate in the flesh, discarding the skin. Add the chili flakes, smash, pit and tear in the olives, mix well, and season to perfection with sea salt and black pepper.

4 Use tongs to remove the garlic bulb from the small drawer, then squeeze the soft flesh into a small bowl, discarding the skin. Mash with the yogurt, ½ tablespoon of extra virgin olive oil and a small squeeze of the other jammy lemon half, reserving it to serve, then season to perfection.

5 Add the eggplant and zucchini to the tomato dressing, pick in the mint and parsley leaves, and toss together. Remove the onions from the air fryer, pull apart into petals and scatter over the top. Crumble on the feta.

6 Serve with the reserved jammy lemon half for squeezing over and with the garlicky yogurt. Great with flatbreads (see page 21) for dunking.

ENERGY	FAT	SAT FAT	PROTEIN	CARBS	SUGARS	SALT	FIBER
331kcal	22.8g	5.9g	10.2g	24.1g	14g	0.7g	7.4g

Avocado fries are a revelation

And they're totally polarizing – they'll definitely get a conversation going! Give them a try, and cook them for your mates. There's just one question: are you a lover or a hater?

 Hands on 5 minutes   **Cook 15 minutes**   **1 Drawer**

Halve, pit and peel **ripe avocados**, then cut into wedges. Gently toss with **fine semolina**, a little seasoning and a **spice of your choice** until coated – smoked paprika, ras el hanout, garam masala or baharat will all work great. Place the fries in a single layer in the air fryer and cook for 15 minutes at 400°F, or until golden, shaking gently halfway. Serve with **yogurt** rippled with **harissa or chili sauce** for dunking. Happy days!

Stuffed squash & black beans

 Serves 2    **Hands on 13 minutes**    **Cook 50 minutes**   **1 Drawer**

2 large butternut squash
bulb ends (about 1¼ lb each)

1 small red onion

2 fresh green chilies

1 x 15-oz can of black beans

1 egg

2 oz feta cheese

2 tbsp couscous

1 bunch of cilantro (about 1 oz)

1 ripe avocado

1 lime

1 Cut the neck ends off the squash and keep for another day (see recipes on pages 75, 87, 93, 123). Use a spoon to scrape out and discard the seeds (there's no need to peel them), then rub all over with olive oil, sea salt and black pepper. Place them in the air-fryer drawer and cook for 20 minutes at 350°F.

2 Peel and quarter the onion and prick the chilies. When the time's up, flip the squash, add the onion and chilies, and cook for another 10 minutes at 350°F.

3 Now, carefully remove all the veg and the shelf. Pour the beans and half their juice into the drawer with 1 tablespoon each of olive oil and red wine vinegar, and a pinch of seasoning. Slice the onion and chilies (seed, if you like), stir into the beans, carefully replace the shelf, and cook for 10 minutes at 325°F.

4 Meanwhile, in a bowl, whisk the egg until light and foamy, then crumble in the feta and add the couscous. Finely chop the cilantro leaves, reserving a few nice ones, and add half to the mix. Pour into the squash bulbs, return them to the drawer and cook, with the beans, for a final 10 minutes at 325°F.

5 Halve, pit, peel and chop the avocado, then dress with half the lime juice and a little drizzle of extra virgin olive oil and season to perfection.

6 Remove the stuffed squash and shelf from the air fryer, then stir the rest of the chopped cilantro into the beans, season to perfection, and divide between plates. Top with the squash, add the dressed avo and reserved cilantro leaves, and serve with lime wedges.

ENERGY	FAT	SAT FAT	PROTEIN	CARBS	SUGARS	SALT	FIBER
571kcal	23g	6.7g	24.1g	65g	31.6g	1.8g	24g

Spicy lime-spiked bok choy

🍽 Serves 2   🔪 Hands on 1 minute   🕐 Cook 15 minutes   🖭 1 Drawer

Quarter **2 baby bok choy** lengthwise, halve **1 lime**, place it all in the air-fryer drawer and toss with a drizzle of olive oil and a pinch of sea salt. Cook for 15 minutes at 350°F, or until the leaves start to char and get gnarly and the core softens, shaking halfway. Transfer to your plates, use tongs to squeeze over the jammy lime juice, and serve drizzled with **1 tablespoon of crunchy peanut & sesame chili oil or salsa macha**. Great in a noodle salad, or paired with tofu or shrimp.

ENERGY	FAT	SAT FAT	PROTEIN	CARBS	SUGARS	SALT	FIBER
81kcal	6.6g	1g	1.9g	2.3g	1.8g	0.7g	2.2g

Sesame snow peas

 Serves 2   Hands on 1 minute   Cook 8–10 minutes   1 Drawer

Remove the shelf from the air-fryer drawer, add **6 oz of snow peas**, then toss with **1 tablespoon of oyster sauce** and **1 tablespoon of toasted sesame oil**. Sprinkle with **1 tablespoon of sesame seeds** and cook for 8 to 10 minutes at 350°F, or until the seeds have toasted and the snow peas are soft and starting to char. Nice with noodles, or salmon, or both!

ENERGY	FAT	SAT FAT	PROTEIN	CARBS	SUGARS	SALT	FIBER
121kcal	9g	1.3g	3.9g	6.3g	5g	0.4g	1.3g

Really good roasted potatoes

 Serves 4   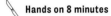 Hands on 8 minutes   Cook 60 minutes   1 Drawer

2 lb medium
Yukon Gold potatoes

4 cloves of garlic

3 tbsp soft unsalted butter

2 sprigs of sage

1 Peel the potatoes, keeping them whole and ideally all about the same size (3 to 3½ inches). Parboil in a pan of boiling salted water for 15 minutes, then drain in a colander and let steam dry for 2 minutes. Give the colander a few light shakes to rough up the edges of the spuds, then tip them back into the pan.

2 Preheat the air fryer to 350°F for 2 minutes. Toss the potatoes with the unpeeled garlic cloves, butter, 1 tablespoon of olive oil and a pinch each of sea salt and black pepper, then evenly space them in the drawer and cook for 30 minutes, or until crisp and golden.

3 Now for the game changer. Pull out the drawer and gently half-squash each potato with a spatula or masher so they kind of push into each other. Pick the sage leaves, toss with a little oil, sprinkle over the potatoes and cook for another 15 minutes, or until super golden and delicious. Squeeze the soft garlic cloves out of their skins and sprinkle with all the lovely crispy bits from the bottom of the drawer before serving.

ENERGY	FAT	SAT FAT	PROTEIN	CARBS	SUGARS	SALT	FIBER
297kcal	12g	5.8g	5.5g	44.3g	1.6g	0.6g	3.3g

You'd better believe it, the air fryer

makes the salad party rock. Get involved

Super salads

Roasted carrot & goat cheese salad

 Serves 2    **Hands on 9 minutes**   **Cook 20 minutes**   **2 Drawer**

12 oz carrots

1 heaping tbsp harissa paste

2 flatbreads or naan

1 x 3-oz round of rinded goat cheese

1½ cups seedless red or black grapes

1 bunch of soft herbs (about 1 oz), such as cilantro, tarragon and Italian parsley

1 small ripe avocado

1 Wash the carrots and halve or quarter lengthwise, depending on their size. Place in the large air-fryer drawer and toss with the harissa, 1 tablespoon of olive oil and a pinch each of sea salt and black pepper. Cook for 20 minutes at 350°F, or until tender, shaking halfway. Add the flatbreads to warm through for the last couple of minutes.

2 Cut the goat cheese in half across the middle and place in the small drawer with the grapes alongside (leave them on the stems, for ease). Drizzle with a little oil, season, and cook for 8 minutes at 350°F, or until the grapes are starting to burst and the cheese is golden and melty.

3 Carefully pick the grapes into a bowl, lightly crush some of them with a fork, pick in the herb leaves, toss with 1 tablespoon each of red wine vinegar and extra virgin olive oil, and season to perfection.

4 Put the warm flatbreads on your plates, halve, pit and peel the avo then smash onto the breads with a fork. Spoon on the grape and herb salad, then top with the harissa carrots and oozy goat cheese, drizzling on any remaining dressing to serve.

ENERGY	FAT	SAT FAT	PROTEIN	CARBS	SUGARS	SALT	FIBER
657kcal	36.8g	10.1g	15.5g	66.8g	24.1g	2.4g	8.7g

Warm panzanella

 Serves 2   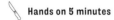 Hands on 5 minutes    Cook 15 minutes   1 Drawer

2 large slices of sourdough bread

1 lb vine-ripe or heirloom tomatoes

1 fat clove of garlic

½ a bunch of oregano (about ⅓ oz) or 1 tsp dried oregano

1 small red onion

2 tsp drained capers

½ a bunch of basil (about ½ oz)

1. Remove the shelf from the air-fryer drawer, lay the bread in the base, then replace the shelf. Cook for 5 minutes at 400°F.

2. Roughly chop the tomatoes, put into a serving bowl, peel and finely grate in the garlic, strip in the oregano, add ½ tablespoon of olive oil and a small pinch each of sea salt and black pepper, and toss well. Tip into the drawer, reserving the bowl for later, and cook for 10 minutes at 400°F, or until softened.

3. Meanwhile, peel and very thinly slice the red onion, then, in the serving bowl, massage it with a pinch of salt and 1 tablespoon of red wine vinegar and let sit to lightly pickle. When the time's up, add the tomatoes to the bowl, then use tongs to carefully remove the shelf and tear the bread into the mix.

4. Add the capers, tear in the basil leaves, add 1 tablespoon of extra virgin olive oil, mix together and season to perfection. If you can resist, let it sit for a few minutes so the flavors can develop, then enjoy.

ENERGY	FAT	SAT FAT	PROTEIN	CARBS	SUGARS	SALT	FIBER
232kcal	10.4g	1.6g	5.8g	29.2g	11.6g	0.9g	4g

Gnarly mushroom & noodle salad

 Serves 2   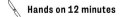 **Hands on 12 minutes**   **Cook 15 minutes**   **1 Drawer**

1 lb mixed mushrooms, such as shiitake and oyster

12 oz fresh thick udon noodles (or cooked, drained udon noodles)

4 scallions

1 English cucumber

½ a bunch of mint (about ½ oz)

1 clove of garlic

1½-inch piece of ginger

1 lime

1 fresh red chili

2 tbsp reduced-sodium soy sauce

1 tbsp fish sauce

1 tbsp toasted sesame seeds

1 Place the mushrooms in the large air-fryer drawer, tearing any larger ones, and cook for 10 minutes at 350°F.

2 Separate the noodles, toss with a spritz of olive oil, then scatter over the mushrooms and cook for another 5 minutes at 350°F, or until heated through.

3 Meanwhile, trim and thinly slice the scallions, roughly chop the cucumber and chop the mint leaves. Peel the garlic and ginger and finely grate into a large bowl with the lime zest, seed, finely chop and add the chili, mix in 2 tablespoons of olive oil, the soy and fish sauces and the lime juice, then season to perfection with sea salt and black pepper to make your dressing.

4 Add the mushrooms and noodles to the dressing, add the scallions, cucumber and mint, toss well, then plate up, finishing with the sesame seeds.

Go vegan
Simply omit the fish sauce to make this vegan.

ENERGY	FAT	SAT FAT	PROTEIN	CARBS	SUGARS	SALT	FIBER
481kcal	20.2g	3.1g	19.5g	54.1g	6.2g	1.8g	7.6g

Curried chicken salad

 Serves 2    **Hands on 12 minutes**    **Cook 40 minutes**   **1 Drawer**

½ x 15-oz can of sliced peaches in juice

2 red onions

2 chicken legs

1 lemon

2 heaping tbsp of your favorite curry paste

6 tbsp sliced almonds

¼ cup Greek yogurt

2 little gem lettuces

1 bunch of cilantro (about 1 oz)

1 fresh red chili

1 Remove the shelf from the air-fryer drawer, spoon the peaches into the base, reserving the juice, and replace the shelf. Peel the onions, cut each into 6 wedges and scatter into the drawer. Pat the chicken legs dry with paper towels, squeeze on half the lemon juice, then rub with the curry paste and 1 tablespoon of olive oil. Put into the drawer, skin-side down, tucking the onions underneath, and cook for 40 minutes at 350°F, or until golden and cooked through, turning halfway, and adding the almonds for the last 5 minutes.

2 Transfer the almonds, chicken and onions to your board and carefully remove the shelf. Stir the yogurt and a splash of the reserved peach juice into the peaches to make the dressing, then shred and add the chicken and crispy skin, discarding the bones, along with the onions, separating into petals as you go. Toss together, then season to perfection with sea salt and black pepper.

3 Cut the lettuces into thin wedges and arrange on a platter, then roughly chop and sprinkle on most of the cilantro leaves. Pile the dressed chicken and onions on top. Thinly slice and add the chili, sprinkle with the almonds and remaining cilantro leaves and serve. Nice with pappadams on the side.

ENERGY	FAT	SAT FAT	PROTEIN	CARBS	SUGARS	SALT	FIBER
572kcal	37.9g	7.7g	31.1g	29.8g	23.1g	1.3g	9.7g

Warm salmon niçoise

 Serves 2    Hands on 10 minutes   Cook 12 minutes   2 Drawer

8 oz green beans

8 oz asparagus

1 little gem lettuce

2 x 5-oz salmon fillets, skin on, scaled, pin-boned

2 medium eggs

1 x 4-inch piece of French baguette (about 2 oz)

1 ripe tomato

8 kalamata olives, with pits

1 tsp Dijon mustard

1 Trim the green beans, snap the woody ends off the asparagus and quarter the little gem lengthwise. Place it all in the large air-fryer drawer with the salmon fillets, drizzle with 1 tablespoon of olive oil, season with sea salt and black pepper and toss to coat. Pull the salmon to the top, skin-side up, and cook for 12 minutes at 400°F, or until the salmon is just cooked, the skin is crispy and the veg have softened.

2 Meanwhile, soft-boil the eggs in boiling water for 6 minutes, then cool in cold water. Peel and set aside. Thinly slice the baguette, then place in the small drawer and cook for 4 minutes at 400°F, or until golden and crisp.

3 To make the dressing, halve the tomato and finely grate into a large shallow bowl, discarding the skin. Smash and pit the olives, then finely chop and add to the bowl along with the mustard, 2 tablespoons of red wine vinegar and 1 tablespoon of extra virgin olive oil. Mix together, then season to perfection.

4 Use tongs to transfer the veg and toasts to the bowl of dressing, toss to coat, flake in the salmon and crispy skin, halve and add the eggs, and serve.

ENERGY	FAT	SAT FAT	PROTEIN	CARBS	SUGARS	SALT	FIBER
565kcal	25.2g	6g	41.4g	21.1g	7.4g	1.5g	5.6g

Spiced potato & chickpea salad

 Serves 2    Hands on 11 minutes    Cook 20 minutes   1 Drawer

1½ x 14½-oz cans of peeled new potatoes (or 15 oz of peeled, cooked potatoes)

2 cloves of garlic

2 tsp cumin seeds

1 x 15-oz can of chickpeas

½ an English cucumber

½ a bunch of mint (about ½ oz)

⅓ cup plain yogurt

1 lime

2 tbsp mango chutney

1 handful of Bombay mix (optional)

1 Line the air-fryer shelf with parchment paper. Drain the potatoes, tip into the drawer and squash with a potato masher. Peel, thinly slice and add the garlic, add the cumin seeds, 2 tablespoons of olive oil and a good pinch each of sea salt and black pepper, then toss to coat. Cook for 10 minutes at 400°F.

2 Drain and add the chickpeas, give it all a good shake, and cook for another 10 minutes at 400°F, or until everything is golden and crisp.

3 Quarter the cucumber lengthwise, remove the seedy core, then finely chop. Pick the mint leaves, reserving a few nice baby ones, and finely chop the rest. Put the cucumber and chopped mint into a bowl with the yogurt, finely grate in the lime zest, squeeze in the juice, add 1 tablespoon of extra virgin olive oil, mix well and season to perfection.

4 Divide the crispy potatoes and chickpeas between plates, then spoon on the cucumber yogurt. Add little dollops of mango chutney, then sprinkle with the Bombay mix and reserved baby mint leaves. Delicious!

ENERGY	FAT	SAT FAT	PROTEIN	CARBS	SUGARS	SALT	FIBER
597kcal	40g	4.8g	17g	66.2g	16.8g	1.4g	9.5g

Chicken Caesar

 Serves 2    Hands on 11 minutes   Cook 30 minutes   2 Drawer

2 large bone-in, skin-on
chicken thighs

1 bulb of fennel

1 slice of sourdough
bread (about 2 oz)

4 cloves of garlic

1 oz Parmesan cheese,
plus extra to serve

4 slices of bacon

2 tsp Dijon mustard

2 tsp Worcestershire sauce

2 tbsp Greek yogurt

½ a lemon

2 little gem or
1 Romaine lettuce

1 Rub the chicken with 1 tablespoon of olive oil and a pinch each of sea salt and black pepper, then cook skin-side up in the large air-fryer drawer for 30 minutes at 400°F, or until golden and cooked through. Trim and thinly slice the fennel, reserving any fronds, and scatter in for the last 10 minutes.

2 Remove the shelf from the small drawer. Tear in the bread in small chunks, add the whole unpeeled garlic cloves, finely grate on half the Parmesan, add 1 tablespoon of oil, season with pepper, toss well, tuck in the bacon and cook for 20 minutes at 400°F, or until golden and crispy, shaking halfway.

3 To make the dressing, finely grate the remaining Parmesan into a large bowl. Squeeze and mash in the soft garlic, discarding the skins. Add the mustard, Worcestershire sauce and yogurt, squeeze in the lemon juice, add 2 tablespoons of extra virgin olive oil and mix well, then season to perfection, loosening with a splash of water, if needed.

4 On your board, remove and reserve the crispy chicken skin, then shred the meat into the dressing, discarding the bones. Separate out the lettuce leaves, tear into the bowl, add the fennel, toss gently to coat, then divide between plates. Crumble on the chicken skin and crispy bacon, and sprinkle with the croutons. Finish with any reserved fennel fronds.

ENERGY	FAT	SAT FAT	PROTEIN	CARBS	SUGARS	SALT	FIBER
488kcal	32.4g	8.8g	28.1g	21.2g	8.4g	1.7g	6g

Duck & couscous salad

 Serves 2    Hands on 12 minutes   Cook 10 minutes, plus resting   1 Drawer

¾ cup whole wheat couscous

1 large carrot (about 5 oz)

2 tbsp dried cranberries

1 large orange

2 x 5-oz duck breast
fillets, skin on

2 tsp ras el hanout

1 red onion

1 clove of garlic

3 tbsp Greek yogurt

4 sprigs of mint

1 tbsp shelled
unsalted pistachios

1 Place the couscous in a large bowl, peel and grate in the carrot, then finely chop and add the cranberries. Finely grate in the orange zest, squeeze in the juice, add 1 tablespoon of red wine vinegar, 2 tablespoons of extra virgin olive oil and enough boiling water to just cover the couscous. Stir, cover and let sit to rehydrate.

2 Pat the duck breasts dry with paper towels and score the skin a few times with a sharp knife, then rub with a little olive oil, sea salt and black pepper and the ras el hanout. Peel the onion and slice into ¼-inch-thick rounds.

3 Use a heatproof ramekin or two metal cookie cutters to raise the air-fryer shelf up (meaning you'll get crispier duck skin), then arrange the onion rounds on the shelf in a single layer. Place the duck on top, skin-side up, and cook for 10 minutes at 400°F, or until crispy on the outside but still pink in the middle. Remove and let rest for 5 minutes, leaving the onions in the drawer to keep warm.

4 Peel the garlic and finely grate into the yogurt. Pick and finely chop the mint leaves, stir half into the yogurt along with a drizzle of extra virgin olive oil, and season to perfection. Mix the rest of the mint into the couscous, season to perfection, then divide between plates with the yogurt. Add the soft onions, then slice and add the duck. Chop and sprinkle on the pistachios to finish.

ENERGY	FAT	SAT FAT	PROTEIN	CARBS	SUGARS	SALT	FIBER
879kcal	36g	8g	54.5g	85.5g	26.4g	2g	13.1g

Squash, grain & mozzarella salad

 Serves 2   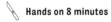 **Hands on 8 minutes**   **Cook 38 minutes**   **1 Drawer**

½ a butternut squash (about 1¼ lb)

1 good pinch of ground cinnamon

1 pinch of dried red chili flakes

1 x 8½-oz package of cooked mixed grains

1 endive

1 little gem lettuce

½ a bunch of mint (about ½ oz)

½ a lemon

1 x 4-oz ball of mozzarella

2 tbsp balsamic glaze

1 Cut the squash into generous 1-inch chunks (peel first, if you like), seeding if necessary. Place in the air-fryer drawer and toss with the cinnamon, chili flakes, 1 tablespoon of olive oil and a pinch each of sea salt and black pepper. Cook for 30 minutes at 350°F, or until soft and caramelized, shaking halfway.

2 Carefully remove the shelf, tipping the squash into the drawer. Sprinkle in the grains and cook for 8 minutes at 350°F, so the grains get crisp and toasty.

3 Thinly slice the endive core, then separate the leaves. Separate out the little gem leaves, thinly slicing any larger leaves, then arrange both on a nice serving platter. Pick over the mint leaves and squeeze on the lemon juice.

4 Spoon the crispy grains and soft squash over the top, then tear on the mozzarella. Drizzle with the balsamic and 1 tablespoon of extra virgin olive oil, season to perfection and serve.

ENERGY	FAT	SAT FAT	PROTEIN	CARBS	SUGARS	SALT	FIBER
693kcal	36.3g	12.1g	27g	66g	22g	1.2g	10.4g

**Easy, delicious, impressive dishes to make
and share with your nearest and dearest**

A little bit fancy

Kerala-style roast chicken & curry sauce

 Serves 6    Hands on 13 minutes    Cook 50 minutes   2 Drawer

1 x 3½-lb whole chicken

1 small head of cauliflower (about 1¼ lb)

4 tbsp Kerala-style curry paste

1 x 24½-oz jar of chickpeas (or 1½ x 15-oz cans of chickpeas)

1 onion

2 cloves of garlic

2-inch piece of ginger

1 fresh red chili

1 bunch of cilantro (about 1 oz)

1 heaping tsp mustard seeds

1 tsp ground turmeric

1 small handful of curry leaves

12 oz (about 2½ cups) ripe cherry tomatoes

1 x 13½-oz can of lite coconut milk

1 lemon

1 Press down firmly on the chicken breasts to break the backbone, squashing the bird slightly, then slash each thigh a few times with a sharp knife. Cut the cauliflower into 6 wedges, discarding any shriveled outer leaves. Rub the chicken and cauliflower all over with 2 tablespoons each of curry paste and olive oil, a little red wine vinegar and a pinch each of sea salt and black pepper.

2 Place the chicken, breast-side down, in the large air-fryer drawer and press down. Cook for 50 minutes at 400°F, or until cooked through, turning halfway.

3 Place the cauliflower in the small drawer and cook for 50 minutes at 400°F, draining and adding the chickpeas halfway through.

4 Meanwhile, for the sauce, peel the onion, garlic and ginger, seed the chili, then thinly slice it all. Finely chop the cilantro stems, reserving the leaves.

5 Place a large non-stick frying pan over medium heat and add 1 tablespoon of oil, the spices and the curry leaves. Fry for 2 minutes, then add the onion, garlic, ginger, chili, a pinch of black pepper, the cilantro stems and the tomatoes. Stir in the remaining 2 tablespoons of curry paste and cook for 15 minutes, or until softened, stirring occasionally.

6 Stir in the coconut milk, then simmer over medium-low heat until reduced to a saucy consistency. Season to perfection with salt, pepper and lemon juice.

7 Transfer the cooked chicken to a platter with the cauliflower and chickpeas, pour on the curry sauce, and finish with the cilantro leaves. Great with fluffy lemon rice, pomegranate-spiked mango chutney, raita and pappadams.

ENERGY	FAT	SAT FAT	PROTEIN	CARBS	SUGARS	SALT	FIBER
494kcal	24.8g	7.5g	45.3g	24.2g	8.5g	1.1g	7.8g

Posh fish & chips

 Serves 2    Hands on 22 minutes    Cook 30 minutes   2 Drawer

1 lb russet potatoes

1 egg

½ tsp smoked paprika

½ oz Parmesan cheese

1 thick slice of seeded
whole wheat bread
(about 1½ oz)

2 x 5-oz skinless salmon
fillets, scaled, pin-boned

1 tbsp all-purpose flour

1 x 12-oz jar of cornichons

1 cup frozen peas

2 sprigs of mint

1 Scrub the potatoes, cut lengthwise into ¾-inch wedges, place in the large air-fryer drawer, toss with 1 tablespoon of olive oil and a pinch each of sea salt and black pepper and arrange in a single layer. Cook for 30 minutes at 400°F, or until golden and cooked through, shaking halfway.

2 Beat the egg with the paprika and a little seasoning in a shallow bowl. Finely grate the Parmesan into a food processor, tear in the bread, add 1 tablespoon of oil and blitz into fine crumbs, then spread onto a plate.

3 Dust the salmon with the flour, then dip into the egg mixture, letting any excess drip off. Coat in the breadcrumbs, spending a bit of time really patting them on. Evenly space in the small drawer and cook for 10 minutes at 400°F, or until golden and just cooked through.

4 Meanwhile, to make the pickle sauce, empty the jar of cornichons and half the juice into the food processor and blitz until smooth. Spoon out 2 portions, then pour the rest back into the jar and keep in the fridge for up to 2 weeks for future meals.

5 Cook the peas for 4 minutes in boiling salted water, then drain, reserving a little cooking water. Tip them into the food processor (there's no need to clean it), pick in the mint leaves and blitz, loosening with splashes of reserved cooking water, if needed, then season to perfection and cover to keep warm.

6 Serve up the fish and chips with the minty peas and pickle sauce.

ENERGY	FAT	SAT FAT	PROTEIN	CARBS	SUGARS	SALT	FIBER
725kcal	22.4g	4.4g	64.6g	69.8g	5.4g	0.9g	8.9g

Oozy Camembert & rainbow dippers

 Serves 4    Hands on 10 minutes   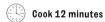 Cook 12 minutes   1 Drawer

1 round of Camembert
(about 8 oz)

½–1 fresh red chili

2 sprigs of thyme

2 large slices of
sourdough bread

1 tbsp runny honey

1½ lb crunchy veg, such as
snow peas, celery, endive,
cucumber, radishes,
bell peppers and fennel

1 clove of garlic

1 Leaving it in the box but removing any paper, cut the rind off the top of the Camembert, leaving a ½-inch rim around the edge. Thinly slice the chili (seed if you like), then poke the slices into the top of the cheese. Strip over the thyme leaves, spritz with a little olive oil, then season with a little pinch each of sea salt and black pepper and place the box of cheese in the air-fryer drawer.

2 Cut the bread into chunky soldiers, arrange around the cheese, spritz with oil and cook for 10 minutes at 350°F. Drizzle the honey over the cheese and cook for a final 2 minutes, or until oozy and the bread is golden.

3 Meanwhile, trim your crunchy veg as needed and cut it all into nice-size pieces perfect for dipping. Pile up on a platter or board.

4 Halve the garlic clove and rub the cut side across the hot toast, add to the platter with the baked cheese and get dunking!

ENERGY	FAT	SAT FAT	PROTEIN	CARBS	SUGARS	SALT	FIBER
264kcal	13g	8.6g	16.5g	20.4g	10g	1.2g	1.3g

Pork & apple pies

 Serves 4   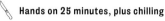 Hands on 25 minutes, plus chilling    Cook 25 minutes   1 Drawer

1½ cups bread flour, plus extra for dusting

8 tbsp cold unsalted butter

1 onion

2 small apples

1 jar (about 8 oz) of piccalilli or other sweet pickle relish

8 oz ground pork

1 egg

4 tsp sesame seeds

1 oz Cheddar cheese

1   Put the flour into a bowl with a pinch of sea salt, then chop and add the butter, rubbing it in with your thumbs and fingertips. Make a well in the middle, gradually mix in 5 tablespoons of cold water, then pat and bring it together into a slightly tacky dough. Wrap and chill in the fridge for 1 hour.

2   Peel the onion, quarter and core the apples, then thinly slice both. Remove the shelf from the air-fryer drawer, add the onion and apples, cook for 10 minutes at 400°F, then remove and let cool. Replace the shelf.

3   Spoon the piccalilli into a blender and blitz until fairly smooth. Put 2 table-spoons into a bowl with the pork and a pinch each of salt and black pepper, put some into a cute dipping bowl for later, then pour the rest back into the jar and keep in the fridge for up to 3 weeks for future meals.

4   Once cool, chop the apple and onion, then add to the pork and massage it all together really well. Divide and flatten into 4 equal rounds. Cut the dough into 4 equal pieces, then, one by one, roll out between two sheets of parchment paper until just under ¼ inch thick and about 6 inches wide. Place one of the rounds of filling in the center of each piece of pastry, then bring the pastry up at the edges to hug the filling, folding and tucking it around in waves and crimps, and leaving some of the filling exposed.

5   Beat the egg, eggwash the exposed pastry, and sprinkle the sesame seeds onto the pastry only. Grate the cheese and sprinkle it over the exposed filling, then lift the pies into the air-fryer drawer and cook for 15 minutes at 400°F, or until the pastry is golden and the filling is cooked through.

6   Serve with the blitzed piccalilli. Great with a carrot, apple and walnut salad.

ENERGY	FAT	SAT FAT	PROTEIN	CARBS	SUGARS	SALT	FIBER
633kcal	35.3g	19.6g	23.7g	58.9g	9.6g	1.6g	3.3g

Golden duck & sweet onion gnocchi

 Serves 2    Hands on 8 minutes   Cook 1 hour 15 minutes   1 Drawer

1 bulb of garlic

2 small red onions

2 small duck legs

½ a bunch of thyme
(about ⅓ oz)

½ a bunch of mint
(about ½ oz)

½ a fresh red chili

1 lb potato gnocchi

8 oz ripe cherry tomatoes
on the vine

1 Remove the shelf from the air-fryer drawer. Halve the unpeeled garlic bulb through the middle. Peel the onions and slice into ½-inch-thick rounds. Pat the duck dry with paper towels, then place it all in the drawer. Strip in the thyme, and toss with 1 tablespoon of olive oil and a pinch each of sea salt and black pepper. Arrange the garlic cut-side down, pull the duck legs to the top, skin-side down, tucking the onions underneath, and cook for 45 minutes at 300°F.

2 Pick the mint leaves and finely chop with the chili, then, in a small bowl, dress with 1 tablespoon each of red wine vinegar and extra virgin olive oil, loosening with a splash of water. Season to perfection.

3 When the time's up on the duck, sprinkle in the gnocchi. Pull the duck legs to the top, skin-side up, and cook for 30 minutes at 350°F, adding the vines of tomatoes for the last 15 minutes.

4 Plate up the duck and tomatoes, then mix the gnocchi and onions in the drawer to soak up the cooking juices, squeezing out the soft garlic cloves and discarding the skins. Pile alongside the duck and serve with the chili-mint sauce.

ENERGY	FAT	SAT FAT	PROTEIN	CARBS	SUGARS	SALT	FIBER
711kcal	24.2g	6g	43.8g	78.7g	10.7g	1.9g	9.2g

Chicken & mushroom pastry parcels

 Serves 2   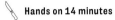 Hands on 14 minutes    Cook 35 minutes   1 Drawer

4 oz mixed mushrooms

1 clove of garlic

4 sprigs of Italian parsley

½ tbsp soft unsalted butter

½ a lemon

2 x 5-oz boneless, skinless chicken breasts

1 sheet of puff pastry (about 7 x 9 inches)

1 egg

2 tsp grainy mustard

⅓ cup dry white wine

⅓ cup heavy cream

1   Tear up any larger mushrooms, then place them all in the air-fryer drawer and toss with 1 tablespoon of olive oil and the unpeeled garlic clove. Cook for 15 minutes at 400°F, or until golden.

2   Tip the golden mushrooms onto a cutting board, squeeze out the soft garlic flesh, discarding the skin, then finely chop it all together. Finely chop the parsley, stems and all, then add to the mixture along with the butter and a squeeze of lemon juice. Season to perfection with sea salt and black pepper and let cool completely.

3   Use the tip of a sharp knife to carefully slice into the thickest part of the chicken breasts horizontally, then open each one up like a book. Add half the cooled mushroom mixture to each breast, then shape back into their original form, sealing the mixture inside.

4   Halve the pastry lengthwise. Stretching each piece slightly, wrap around the chicken. Beat the egg and brush it all over, then place the parcels in the drawer. Cook for 20 minutes at 400°F, or until golden and cooked through.

5   For the sauce, place a non-stick frying pan over medium-high heat and add the mustard and wine. Simmer until reduced by half, then add the cream and simmer until the sauce coats the back of a spoon. Season to perfection and divide between plates.

6   Slice each chicken parcel and place it on top of the sauce, drizzling on any juices from the bottom of the drawer and finishing with a drizzle of extra virgin olive oil, if you like. Delicious with roasted carrots and watercress.

ENERGY	FAT	SAT FAT	PROTEIN	CARBS	SUGARS	SALT	FIBER
725kcal	42.4g	19.1g	45.7g	34.4g	2.3g	0.7g	1.9g

Gnarly pork & pineapple noodles

 Serves 4    Hands on 20 minutes   Cook 35 minutes   2 Drawer

1 small pineapple (about 1¼ lb)

Chinese five spice powder

1 lb pork belly, thinly sliced

1 red bell pepper

8 oz flat rice noodles (rice linguine)

1 fresh red chili

2½-inch piece of ginger

1 clove of garlic

1 lime

2 tbsp reduced-sodium soy sauce

2 tsp toasted sesame oil

2 tsp fish sauce

1 tbsp + 2 tsp runny honey

1¾ lb crunchy veg, such as cucumber, radishes, sugar snap peas, carrots and asparagus

1 bunch of mint and cilantro (about 1 oz total)

1 tbsp sesame seeds

1 Trim, peel and core the pineapple, then cut into 8 pieces. Sprinkle with a pinch of five spice, drizzle with a little olive oil, then place in the small air-fryer drawer and cook for 30 minutes at 400°F, or until caramelized.

2 Toss the pork belly with 1 tablespoon of oil, 1 teaspoon of five spice and a generous pinch each of sea salt and black pepper. Tear the pepper into quarters, discarding the seeds, then place it all in the large drawer. Cook for 25 minutes at 400°F, or until golden and gnarly.

3 In a bowl, cover the noodles with boiling water and let sit to rehydrate, then drain and refresh under cold running water.

4 To make the dressing, drizzle 2 tablespoons of olive oil onto a serving platter. Finely chop and add the chili. Peel the ginger and garlic, then finely grate on along with the lime zest. Squeeze on the lime juice, add the soy, sesame oil, fish sauce and 2 teaspoons of honey and mix together.

5 Trim and prep the crunchy veg – chop cucumber, radishes and sugar snap peas, and shave carrots and asparagus into ribbons. Pile it all onto the platter with the noodles, and tear on the herb leaves, ready to dress later.

6 When the time's up, remove the pepper pieces from the large drawer and toss into the salad. Add 1 tablespoon of honey and the sesame seeds to the pork, toss to coat, and cook for a final 10 minutes at 400°F, turning halfway.

7 Cut the pork and pineapple into chunks, scatter onto the salad, toss everything together, coating in the dressing, season to perfection and serve.

ENERGY	FAT	SAT FAT	PROTEIN	CARBS	SUGARS	SALT	FIBER
802kcal	43.1g	12.2g	35g	69g	26.6g	1.7g	2.2g

Herb-stuffed salmon & red pepper salsa

 Serves 2    Hands on 8 minutes    Cook 20 minutes   2 Drawer

1½ x 14½-oz cans of peeled new potatoes (or 15 oz of peeled, cooked potatoes)

1 lemon

8 oz asparagus

4 oz green beans

8 oz broccolini

2 x 5-oz salmon fillets, skin on, scaled, pin-boned

½ a bunch of mixed soft herbs (about ½ oz), such as dill, basil, Italian parsley and mint

2 large jarred roasted red peppers

2 tsp drained capers

½ a small clove of garlic

½ tsp Dijon mustard

1 Drain the potatoes, halving any larger ones. Slice half the lemon into thin rounds, then place it all in the small air-fryer drawer, tucking the lemon slices underneath. Spritz with olive oil, season with sea salt and black pepper, and cook for 20 minutes at 400°F, or until golden and crisp, shaking halfway.

2 Snap the woody ends off the asparagus, place the spears in the large drawer, then trim and add the green beans. Trim the broccolini, halving any thicker stems lengthwise, and scatter into the drawer, then add a splash of water (or white wine, if you have some open!) and cook for 4 minutes at 400°F.

3 While your veg gets a head start, pinch the salmon fillets and – with a sharp knife – carefully slice down into the skin lengthwise, about ½ inch deep. Season with salt and pepper, then pick and stuff in half the herb leaves, as well as a few gratings of lemon zest. Place on top of the green veg, skin-side up, spritz everything with oil, then cook for 8 minutes at 400°F, or until the salmon and veg are cooked through.

4 To make the salsa, place the peppers and capers on a board. Peel and finely grate on the garlic, then very finely chop it all, mixing as you go. Dress with the mustard and a squeeze of lemon juice, and season to perfection.

5 Divide the lemony potatoes between plates, then add the green veg and salmon, drizzling on any juices from the large drawer. Pick over the remaining herb leaves and finish with the salsa.

ENERGY	FAT	SAT FAT	PROTEIN	CARBS	SUGARS	SALT	FIBER
453kcal	17g	2.9g	38.2g	36g	9.4g	1.7g	7.8g

Harissa roasted cauli

 Serves 2    **Hands on 9 minutes**    **Cook 40 minutes**   **2 Drawer**

1 head of cauliflower (about 2 lb)

2 tbsp harissa paste

2 tbsp sliced almonds

2 tbsp sesame seeds

1 tbsp cumin seeds

1 tsp coriander seeds

½ cup whole wheat couscous

1 lemon

½ a bunch of mint (about ½ oz)

½ a bunch of Italian parsley (about ½ oz)

1 pomegranate

generous ¼ cup Greek yogurt

1 Remove the shelf from each air-fryer drawer. Trim the cauliflower, remove and discard only the shriveled outer leaves, then cut into 6 wedges and place in the large drawer. Toss with the harissa, 1 tablespoon of olive oil and a good pinch each of sea salt and black pepper. Cook for 40 minutes at 350°F, turning halfway.

2 In the small drawer, cook the almonds with the sesame, cumin and coriander seeds for 7 minutes at 350°F, or until nicely toasted. Transfer to a mortar and pestle along with a small pinch of salt and pound until fairly fine to make dukkah.

3 Put the couscous into a bowl, finely grate in the lemon zest, season, just cover with boiling water, cover, and set aside. Pick and finely chop most of the herb leaves.

4 After a few minutes, fluff up the couscous with a fork, add the chopped herbs, and squeeze in the lemon juice. Halve the pomegranate, then, holding one half cut-side down in your palm, bash the back of it with a spoon so all the seeds tumble through your fingers into the bowl. Mix it all together.

5 Spread the yogurt onto two serving plates, load the couscous on top, then add the cauliflower wedges and drizzle with any harissa oil from the bottom of the drawer. Sprinkle with some of the dukkah (saving any excess for another day or to use in my Squashage rolls, page 87) and the reserved herb leaves. Holding the remaining pomegranate half cut-side down in your palm, bash the back of it with a spoon so all the seeds tumble over the cauliflower, to finish.

ENERGY	FAT	SAT FAT	PROTEIN	CARBS	SUGARS	SALT	FIBER
549kcal	25.2g	4.9g	23.1g	61.9g	18.4g	0.6g	13.4g

Lemon fish, spuds & spinach sauce

 Serves 2    **Hands on 10 minutes**    **Cook 22 minutes**   **2 Drawer**

1 lb russet potatoes

1 oz Cheddar cheese

1 tsp jarred horseradish

2 tbsp sour cream

8 oz baby spinach

½ a bunch of dill (about ⅓ oz)

1 lemon

2 x 5-oz thick, skinless white fish fillets, pin-boned

1 Scrub the potatoes, chop into ½-inch cubes, place in the large air-fryer drawer and toss with 1½ tablespoons of olive oil and a pinch each of sea salt and black pepper. Cook for 20 minutes at 400°F, or until golden, shaking halfway.

2 Place the cheese, horseradish, sour cream, half the spinach and most of the dill, stems and all, in a blender with ¼ cup of water. Squeeze in one-quarter of the lemon juice and blitz until smooth, then season to perfection. Remove the shelf from the small drawer, then pour in the sauce and replace the shelf.

3 Season the fish fillets and place in the small drawer. Thinly slice 4 rounds of lemon, place on top of the fish, spritz with oil, and cook for 12 to 15 minutes at 325°F, or until the fish is just cooked through and the sauce is hot.

4 Tip the potatoes out of the large drawer and pack in the remaining spinach. Cook for 2 minutes at 400°F, or until just wilted, while you remove the fish from the small drawer so you can divide the sauce between plates. Arrange the fish, potatoes and wilted spinach on top. Pick over the reserved dill and finish with a drizzle of extra virgin olive oil, if you like.

ENERGY	FAT	SAT FAT	PROTEIN	CARBS	SUGARS	SALT	FIBER
488kcal	19g	5.7g	38.7g	42.6g	4.5g	1.5g	3.2g

Sweet pepper lentils & sausages

 Serves 2    Hands on 10 minutes    Cook 30 minutes, plus steaming   2 Drawer

3 mixed-color bell peppers

1–2 fresh red chilies

4 fat cloves of garlic

4 pork sausages

½ a bunch of Italian parsley (about ½ oz)

1 x 10-oz package of cooked lentils

1 Prick the peppers and chilies a few times with a sharp knife, place in the large air-fryer drawer, spritz with olive oil, and cook for 30 minutes at 400°F, or until soft and starting to char, turning halfway and adding the unpeeled garlic cloves. Let it all steam in the drawer for 5 minutes.

2 Hasselback the sausages by cutting deep slits crosswise down their length. Spritz with oil and cook in the small drawer for 20 minutes at 400°F, or until golden and cooked through, shaking halfway.

3 Squeeze the soft garlic onto a large board, discarding the skins. Once cool enough to handle, remove the skin and seeds from the peppers and chilies, adding the flesh to the board. Finely chop with the parsley, stems and all, reserving a few nice leaves, mixing as you go. Reheat the lentils according to the package instructions, then fold in the veg. Dress with 2 tablespoons of red wine vinegar, 1 tablespoon of extra virgin olive oil, and season to perfection with sea salt and black pepper, then divide between plates.

4 Serve with the hasselback sausages, sprinkled with the reserved parsley leaves. Nice with steamed greens or a salad.

Easy swaps

Feel free to use a can of lentils, if you prefer. Once the large drawer is empty, remove the shelf, then simply drain and add the lentils. Heat for 5 minutes at 400°F, or until piping hot.

ENERGY	FAT	SAT FAT	PROTEIN	CARBS	SUGARS	SALT	FIBER
619kcal	39.6g	13.1g	25.9g	41.1g	15.3g	1.5g	16.1g

Because we all love a canapé – tasty handheld bites to share with your mates

Cute canapés

Sesame shrimp toasts

 Makes 8    Hands on 11 minutes   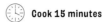 Cook 15 minutes   1 Drawer

2 slices of white bread

2 scallions

¾-inch piece of ginger

6 oz raw peeled jumbo shrimp

1 tbsp reduced-sodium soy sauce

1 medium egg

2 tbsp toasted sesame seeds

1 Pop the bread into the air-fryer drawer and cook for 3 minutes at 400°F, or until one side is golden. You might need to do this in batches.

2 Trim and thinly slice the scallions, putting the green tops aside for garnish. Peel and finely chop the ginger. Add the shrimp to the party, drizzle with the soy, then chop it all together until fairly fine. Crack in the egg and mix to combine (or blitz everything in a food processor, if you prefer).

3 Spread the shrimp mixture on the untoasted sides of the bread right to the edges, then cut each piece into 4 triangles and sprinkle with the sesame seeds. Evenly space in the drawer, in batches if needed, spritz with olive oil, and cook for 12 minutes at 350°F, or until golden and cooked through.

4 Transfer to a serving platter and sprinkle with the reserved scallions. Great with sweet red chili sauce, or your favorite condiment, for dunking.

ENERGY	FAT	SAT FAT	PROTEIN	CARBS	SUGARS	SALT	FIBER
61kcal	2.2g	0.5g	5.6g	4.7g	0.5g	0.4g	0.5g

Mushroom swirls

 Makes 8    **Hands on 10 minutes**    **Cook 20 minutes**   **2 Drawer**

6 oz chestnut or cremini mushrooms

1 clove of garlic

1 sheet of puff pastry (about 7 x 9 inches)

1 egg

smoked paprika

1 oz Cheddar cheese

½ a bunch of chives (about ⅓ oz)

2 tbsp sour cream

1 Trim the mushrooms, quartering any larger ones, place in the small air-fryer drawer, spritz with olive oil, toss to coat, and cook for 10 minutes at 350°F. Peel and thinly slice the garlic, add to the drawer and cook for another 10 minutes at 350°F, or until soft and golden.

2 Unroll the pastry sheet on its paper. Beat the egg and brush all over the surface, sprinkle with a light dusting of paprika and a pinch each of sea salt and black pepper, and finely grate on the cheese. Use the paper to help you roll the pastry up from one of the shorter ends into a log.

3 Cut into 8 equal rounds, turn them onto their cut sides and use the palm of your hand to flatten them into 2½-inch-wide discs, then eggwash the tops. Spritz the shelf in the large drawer with oil, add the pastries, evenly spaced, and cook for 10 minutes at 400°F, or until beautifully golden.

4 Finely chop the chives. Remove the cooked mushrooms and garlic to your board, add most of the chives, then finely chop it all together, mixing as you go. Stir in the sour cream, then season to perfection. Spoon the mushroom mixture onto the pastry swirls and serve sprinkled with the remaining chives.

ENERGY	FAT	SAT FAT	PROTEIN	CARBS	SUGARS	SALT	FIBER
110kcal	7.1g	3.7g	3.1g	8.4g	0.3g	0.1g	0.4g

Nuts for toasty spiced nuts

Nuts go to another flavor dimension when toasted and tossed with nice things – nail that balance between sweet, salty and spicy and you'll be in a great place. Happy snacking!

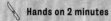 **Hands on 2 minutes**   **Cook 8 minutes**   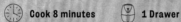 **1 Drawer**

Toss **1⅓ cups of shelled unsalted mixed nuts** in 1 tablespoon of olive oil, **1 tablespoon of runny honey or maple syrup, ½ tablespoon of smoked paprika** and a **generous pinch each of cayenne** and black pepper. Remove the shelf from the air-fryer drawer, tip in the dressed nuts, shake into an even layer, and cook for 8 minutes at 325°F, or until toasted and caramelized, shaking halfway. Tip onto a sheet of parchment paper, sprinkle with a good pinch of sea salt and let cool, then either serve right away or pop into an airtight container for future snacking wins.

Shrimp party skewers

 Makes 8   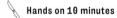 **Hands on 10 minutes**   **Cook 8 minutes**   **1 Drawer**

2 thick slices of
sourdough bread

6 oz raw peeled
jumbo shrimp

4 oz cured chorizo

2 large jarred roasted
red peppers

4 sprigs of Italian parsley

1 clove of garlic

1 pinch of smoked paprika

1 lemon

1 Cut 4 wooden skewers in half, or use little wooden skewers if you've got them, and soak in cold water to prevent burning.

2 Cut the bread into ¾-inch cubes and place in a bowl with the shrimp. Thinly slice the chorizo into rounds and add to the bowl, then cut the peppers into long ¾-inch-thick strips and add to the mix. Pick and finely chop the parsley, stems and all, add most to the bowl, reserving some of the chopped leaves, then peel and finely grate in the garlic. Add a pinch each of paprika and black pepper and 1 tablespoon of olive oil, and toss gently to coat.

3 Skewer the shrimp, bread and chorizo, weaving with the pepper strips among the skewers. Place in the air-fryer drawer and cook for 8 minutes at 400°F, or until golden and the shrimp are cooked through, turning halfway.

4 Sprinkle with the remaining parsley and serve with lemon wedges.

ENERGY	FAT	SAT FAT	PROTEIN	CARBS	SUGARS	SALT	FIBER
115kcal	6.8g	2.2g	7.8g	5.4g	1.1g	0.6g	0.4g

Baked hot honey cheese

Salty cheese, the hum of chili or paprika, and sweet honey are a match made in heaven – the contrast and flavor combo is phenomenal. Don't take my word for it, give it a try and see for yourself. You won't look back.

 Hands on 3 minutes **Cook 15 minutes** **1 Drawer**

Cut crosshatch slits in an **8-oz block of halloumi or feta cheese**, going halfway through. In a small heatproof dish that will snugly fit the cheese, mix together **2 tablespoons of runny honey** and **½ teaspoon of Aleppo pepper or 1 heaping teaspoon of smoked paprika**, then rub it all over the cheese, making sure you get into all the slits. Place the dish in the air-fryer drawer and cook for 15 minutes at 350°F, or until soft, dark and gnarly, basting halfway. Let cool just a little, then serve. Great as it is with nibbles, served on toast, or chopped into chunks and paired with a tomato, red onion and mint salad.

Miso chicken wings

 Makes 8    **Hands on 6 minutes**    **Cook 29 minutes**   **1 Drawer**

8 small whole chicken wings, tips removed

1 tbsp miso paste

1 tbsp runny honey

1 tsp rice wine vinegar

2 scallions

1 tbsp toasted sesame seeds

1 Place the chicken wings in the air-fryer drawer and toss with 2 tablespoons of olive oil and a pinch each of sea salt and black pepper. Cook for 25 minutes at 400°F, or until cooked through, shaking halfway.

2 In a small bowl, mix the miso, honey and vinegar together to make a glaze. Trim and thinly slice the scallions.

3 Brush the chicken wings with half the glaze and cook for another 4 minutes at 350°F, or until dark golden and gnarly, turning halfway and brushing with the remaining glaze when you turn them.

4 Load the wings onto a board or serving platter, sprinkle with the sesame seeds and scallions and dig in. Sticky fingers await!

ENERGY	FAT	SAT FAT	PROTEIN	CARBS	SUGARS	SALT	FIBER
132kcal	8.3g	2.3g	12.8g	2.6g	2.1g	0.3g	0.1g

Smoked haddock pakoras

 Serves 8    Hands on 17 minutes   Cook 15 minutes   1 Drawer

1½ x 14½-oz cans of peeled new potatoes (or 15 oz of peeled, cooked potatoes)

1 tbsp curry powder

5 tbsp chickpea flour

1 small red onion

1 fresh green chili

½ a bunch of cilantro (about ½ oz)

8 oz smoked trout or haddock fillets

½ a bunch of mint (about ½ oz)

½ cup plain yogurt

1 lemon

1 Drain the potatoes, pat dry with paper towels, then crush in a large bowl with the curry powder and chickpea flour. Adding to the bowl as you go, peel and finely dice the onion, thinly slice the chili, finely chop most of the cilantro, stems and all, reserving a few nice leaves, and finely dice the fish.

2 Season with sea salt and black pepper, mix together well, then use clean wet hands to divide and shape into 16 even balls. Evenly space the pakoras in the air-fryer drawer, working in batches if needed, spritz well with olive oil, then cook for 15 minutes at 400°F, or until golden and cooked through.

3 Meanwhile, pick most of the mint leaves into a mortar and pestle, reserving a few baby ones, and pound into a paste with a pinch of salt. Muddle in the yogurt and a good squeeze of lemon juice, and season to perfection. Transfer to a small dipping bowl.

4 Sprinkle the reserved herb leaves over the pakoras, then serve with lemon wedges and the minty yogurt dip for dunking.

ENERGY	FAT	SAT FAT	PROTEIN	CARBS	SUGARS	SALT	FIBER
133kcal	1.8g	0.4g	13.3g	15.8g	2g	1g	1.8g

Sticky sausage skewers

Cocktail sausages are one of those things that just love to be cooked in the air fryer – they get lovely and golden and are perfect for a quick canapé or bite to share with friends.

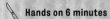 **Hands on 6 minutes**   **Cook 17 minutes**   **1 Drawer**

Halve **slices of bacon** crosswise. Use a toothpick (soaked in cold water to prevent burning) to skewer up a couple of **raw cocktail sausages**, each wrapped in ½ a slice of bacon, interspersing with picked **sage leaves**. Evenly space in the air-fryer drawer and cook for 15 minutes at 350°F, or until golden and cooked through, shaking halfway. Give the sausages another good shake, drizzle with **runny honey** and cook for a final 2 minutes at 350°F, then serve.

Veggie love

Simply ditch the bacon and swap in mini veggie sausages for a veggie twist.

Stuffed olives

 Makes 16   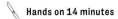 Hands on 14 minutes   Cook 12 minutes   1 Drawer

6 anchovy fillets in oil

2 cloves of garlic

½ a lemon

4 sprigs of Italian parsley

16 large Spanish pitted queen green olives

2 tbsp all-purpose flour

1 egg

2 medium slices of white sandwich bread (about 3 oz)

smoked paprika

1 Place the anchovies on your board, reserving the oil. Peel and add the garlic cloves, finely grate on the lemon zest, add half the parsley leaves and all the stems, then finely chop it all together, mixing as you go (you could use a mini food processor here, if you prefer).

2 Spoon the filling into a sandwich bag, cut off the corner and squeeze into the olives, then coat them in the flour. Beat the egg in a shallow bowl. In a food processor, blitz the bread with 1 tablespoon of the reserved anchovy oil into super-fine crumbs and tip onto a plate. Coat the floured olives in the egg, letting any excess drip off, then roll in the breadcrumbs until evenly coated.

3 Evenly space the olives in the air-fryer drawer and cook for 12 minutes at 350°F, or until golden and crisp, shaking halfway and spritzing with oil, if needed. Finely chop the remaining parsley leaves and sprinkle them on along with the paprika. Serve with lemon wedges.

Veggie love

Sub out the anchovy mixture for 2 oz of sun-dried tomatoes, split between the olives, and use the oil from the sun-dried tomato jar for the breadcrumbs.

ENERGY	FAT	SAT FAT	PROTEIN	CARBS	SUGARS	SALT	FIBER
43kcal	2.6g	0.4g	1.4g	3.8g	0.2g	0.6g	0.1g

Spring rolls & soy dipping sauce

 Makes 8    Hands on 16 minutes   Cook 20 minutes   1 Drawer

¾ oz dried mushrooms

1 medium carrot

2 scallions

1 clove of garlic

¾-inch piece of ginger

6 oz fresh medium noodles
(or cooked, drained noodles)

1 tbsp crunchy peanut
& sesame chili oil
or salsa macha

4 sheets of phyllo pastry

toasted sesame oil

1 tbsp reduced-sodium
soy sauce

1 tsp runny honey

1 tbsp rice wine vinegar

1 Cover the dried mushrooms with 1 cup of boiling water and let sit to rehydrate. Wash and coarsely grate the carrot, trim and thinly slice the scallions, reserving the green tops, then peel and finely grate the garlic and ginger. Place it all in a bowl with the noodles.

2 Reserving the soaking liquid, scoop out the mushrooms, squeeze out excess moisture, finely chop, then stir into the mix along with the chili oil and a pinch of sea salt.

3 Working fairly quickly, cut each phyllo sheet in half crosswise, brush with a little sesame oil, then evenly divide up the noodle mixture at the bottom of each pastry strip. Tuck in the ends, then roll up and brush with more sesame oil.

4 Evenly space the rolls in the air-fryer drawer and cook for 20 minutes at 350°F, or until golden and crisp, cooking in batches if needed.

5 Meanwhile, pour a scant ½ cup of the mushroom soaking liquid into a small non-stick frying pan, discarding the rest. Add the soy and honey and reduce over high heat to a dipping sauce consistency – the mushroom liquid will give incredible depth of flavor. Stir in the rice wine vinegar and reserved scallion tops, then pour into a little bowl. Serve with the spring rolls.

ENERGY	FAT	SAT FAT	PROTEIN	CARBS	SUGARS	SALT	FIBER
108kcal	4.4g	0.6g	3.1g	14.4g	2g	0.4g	1.6g

It's true! You can successfully emulate baking in an air fryer – you gotta try these

Get your bake on

Cheddar cheese & chive scones

 Serves 6    Hands on 16 minutes   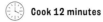 Cook 12 minutes   1 Drawer

1½ cups self-rising flour, plus extra for dusting

1 tsp baking powder

1 tsp dry mustard powder

cayenne pepper

5 tbsp cold unsalted butter

4 oz sharp Cheddar cheese

1 bunch of chives (about ⅔ oz)

5 tbsp milk, plus extra for brushing

8 oz reduced-fat cream cheese

½ a lemon

1 Sift the flour into a bowl with the baking powder and mustard, then add a generous pinch each of cayenne pepper and sea salt. Cube up the butter, then use your thumbs and fingertips to rub it into the flour mixture until you have little cornflake-size pieces.

2 Coarsely grate in 3½ oz of the Cheddar, finely chop and add the chives, then mix everything together. Make a well in the middle, pour in the milk, and bring together into a soft, dry dough, adding a tiny extra splash of milk, if needed – use your hands, if necessary, but don't be tempted to overmix.

3 Turn out onto a lightly floured surface and quickly work the dough into a 1½-inch-thick round, then cut into 6 triangular wedges. Lightly brush the tops with milk, grate on the remaining cheese, and sprinkle with a little cayenne.

4 Rub the air-fryer shelf with a little olive oil, then preheat the air fryer to 350°F for 2 minutes. Add the scones, evenly spaced, and cook for 12 minutes, or until golden – you may need to work in batches.

5 Mix the cream cheese with a few good gratings of lemon zest, season with black pepper, and add a drizzle of extra virgin olive oil, if you like. Serve with the warm scones. Great with a watercress, endive, apple and walnut salad.

Tip: If you don't have self-rising flour, substitute 1½ cups of all-purpose flour plus ¼ teaspoon sea salt and increase the baking powder to 3¼ teaspoons.

ENERGY	FAT	SAT FAT	PROTEIN	CARBS	SUGARS	SALT	FIBER
368kcal	24g	13.7g	11.4g	28.3g	2.9g	1.1g	1.3g

Herby cheese soda bread

 Serves 8–10   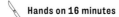 Hands on 16 minutes   Cook 30 minutes   1 Drawer

1½ cups whole wheat flour

1½ cups all-purpose flour, plus extra for dusting

½ cup old-fashioned rolled oats, plus extra for sprinkling

1 heaping tsp baking soda

4 sprigs of rosemary

1 large egg

1¼ cups buttermilk or plain yogurt

4 oz Cheddar cheese

1 In a large bowl, mix together both flours, the oats, baking soda and 1 level teaspoon of sea salt. Pick and finely chop the rosemary leaves and stir most of them into the mixture, reserving the remainder.

2 Make a well in the middle, crack in the egg and add the buttermilk, then mix thoroughly with a fork. Gradually bring in the flour from the outside, then use your clean lightly floured hands to pat and bring the dough together.

3 Chop the cheese into chunks, mix in, then shape the dough into a ball, using your clean oiled hands to flatten it into a disc, roughly 1½ inches thick. Sprinkle with a few extra oats and a little sea salt, patting both onto the dough. Score a deep crosshatch pattern into the top, then carefully place in the air-fryer drawer and cook for 20 minutes at 350°F.

4 Rub the reserved chopped rosemary with 1 teaspoon of olive oil, sprinkle over the bread and cook for another 10 minutes at 350°F, or until a firm crust has formed and the bread sounds hollow when tapped on the bottom.

5 Transfer to a wire cooling rack and serve warm.

ENERGY	FAT	SAT FAT	PROTEIN	CARBS	SUGARS	SALT	FIBER
286kcal	7.3g	3.3g	12.3g	45.9g	3g	1.5g	4.1g

Freezer-stash muffins

 Serves 12   Hands on 10 minutes, plus freezing   Cook 22 minutes   1 Drawer

2 cups self-rising flour

½ cup packed light
brown sugar

¾ cup reduced-fat milk

¾ cup olive oil

1 egg

1 tsp ground cardamom

6 oz carrots

3½ oz white chocolate

1¼ cups old-fashioned
rolled oats

1 Line a 12-cup muffin pan with paper liners, ready to freeze your muffins – the idea here is that we make a whole batch, then freeze them so you can bake them to order, as and when you desire.

2 In a food processor, blitz the flour, sugar, milk, oil, egg, cardamom and a small pinch of sea salt together until smooth. Peel and coarsely grate in the carrots, snap in the chocolate and add the oats. Briefly pulse until the chocolate has broken down into chip-size chunks, so you retain some texture.

3 Divide the batter between the muffin cups, cover and pop the whole tray into the freezer, where they'll keep, covered, for up to 3 months. Once they're frozen, I recommend transferring them to a bag for easy storage.

4 To cook a muffin, simply transfer directly from freezer to air fryer and cook for 22 minutes at 325°F, or until golden and an inserted skewer comes out clean. Cool on a wire rack, then dig in.

Tip: If you don't have self-rising flour, substitute 2 cups of all-purpose flour plus 1 tablespoon baking powder and ½ teaspoon sea salt.

Hungry?

If you want to cook any muffins right away, simply place each filled liner in a heatproof teacup or ramekin to help it hold its shape, and cook in the air fryer for 14 minutes at 325°F.

ENERGY	FAT	SAT FAT	PROTEIN	CARBS	SUGARS	SALT	FIBER
337kcal	18.8g	4g	4.9g	40g	15.1g	0.3g	1.9g

Delicious doughnuts

 Serves 4    Hands on 15 minutes, plus chilling & proofing   Cook 14 minutes   1 Drawer

2 large eggs

1½ cups all-purpose flour, plus extra for dusting

¼ cup sugar

heaping 1 tsp instant dry yeast

7 tbsp soft unsalted butter

1 pinch of ground cinnamon

4 tbsp of your favorite jam, such as strawberry, raspberry, apricot or blackberry

1   Crack the eggs into a food processor, add the flour, ½ tablespoon of sugar, the yeast and a pinch of sea salt, then pulse into a sticky ball of dough. A spoonful at a time, pulse 4 tablespoons of the butter into the mixture, waiting until each spoonful is combined before adding more – this helps to enrich the dough. Lightly dust it with flour, pat into a round, place in a clean bowl, then cover and let rest in the fridge for at least 2 hours, or overnight.

2   Divide the dough into 4 equal pieces on a clean work surface and roll into balls. Transfer to a parchment paper–lined baking sheet, cover, then let sit in a warm place for 1 hour, or until doubled in size.

3   Gently transfer the doughnuts to the air-fryer drawer and cook for 10 minutes at 350°F, or until beautifully golden and fluffy, then remove.

4   For the coating, melt the remaining butter in a heatproof bowl in the air fryer for 4 minutes at 350°F. Mix the remaining sugar with the cinnamon in a shallow bowl. One at a time, roll the warm doughnuts in the butter to coat, then dip straight into the sugar. Let cool, then slice open and spread a tablespoon of jam in the center of each. Heaven.

Feed a crowd

It's easy to double up on this one if you're feeding more people – simply cook the doughnuts in two batches for the best results.

ENERGY	FAT	SAT FAT	PROTEIN	CARBS	SUGARS	SALT	FIBER
465kcal	22.3g	12.6g	8.7g	60.8g	20.9g	0.1g	1.8g

Mint choc chip whoopie pies

 Serves 8   Hands on 10 minutes, plus chilling   Cook 37 minutes   1 Drawer

5 oz mint Aero or other mint-chocolate bar

5 oz cream cheese

6 tbsp unsalted butter

1½ cups self-rising flour

½ cup sugar

3 tbsp unsweetened cocoa powder

½ tsp baking soda

½ cup milk or dark chocolate chips

2 medium eggs

1 To make the filling, snap 4 oz of the mint Aero into a heatproof bowl and melt in the air fryer for 3 minutes at 325°F, then stir until smooth and mix in the cream cheese. Cover and chill in the fridge for at least 1 hour.

2 Melt the butter in a heatproof bowl for 4 minutes at 325°F. In a large bowl, whisk together the flour, sugar, cocoa and baking soda, then stir in the chocolate chips, mix in the melted butter, then the eggs, until the mixture is well combined. With wet hands, roll into 16 balls and place on a lined baking sheet, pressing them down slightly to flatten.

3 Line the air-fryer shelf with parchment paper. Transfer 4 to 6 cookies into the drawer, making sure there's a ½-inch space between them. Cook for 10 minutes at 325°F (12 minutes from chilled or 15 minutes from frozen), then, using the paper to help you, transfer the cookies to a wire rack to cool, and repeat.

4 Once the cookies are completely cool, sandwich them with the filling, crumbling up the leftover mint Aero to sprinkle into each one before sandwiching.

Tip: If you don't have self-rising flour, substitute 1½ cups of all-purpose flour plus 2¼ teaspoons baking powder and ¼ teaspoon sea salt.

Make ahead

If not cooking right away, cover the raw cookies and keep in the fridge for up to 2 days, or the freezer for up to 3 months, ready to cook to order! Or, once cooked, keep them in an airtight container at room temperature for up to 3 days, stashing the filling in the fridge, ready to assemble.

ENERGY	FAT	SAT FAT	PROTEIN	CARBS	SUGARS	SALT	FIBER
451kcal	25g	15.1g	6.7g	52.2g	32.6g	0.6g	1.9g

The wonderful world of whoopie pies

Mint choc chip is an undeniably great combo (see page 181), but really the world of whoopie pies is your oyster, so go to town and see what you come up with. How do you like yours?

Here are some mouthwatering thought starters for you . . .

- Swap the mint chocolate for white chocolate and a grating of orange zest

- Sandwich a scoop of your favorite ice cream in the middle

- Crush frozen raspberries into Greek yogurt for a bit of contrast

- Spread with your favorite toast topping – try marmalade, jam, Biscoff or chocolate-hazelnut spread.

Ginger shortbread

 Serves 12    Hands on 10 minutes, plus chilling   Cook 16 minutes   1 Drawer

10 tbsp soft unsalted butter

1½ cups all-purpose flour

¼ cup sugar, plus extra
for sprinkling

2 oz drained stem
ginger in syrup

2 oz of your favorite chocolate

1 In a bowl, use your thumbs and fingertips to rub together the soft butter, flour, sugar and a pinch of sea salt, then finely chop and add the ginger.

2 Squash and pat into a dough, shape into a large log, wrap in parchment paper and twist the ends to seal. Let firm up in the fridge for at least 20 minutes.

3 Once firm, slice the log into 12 even rounds. At this point, you can bake however many cookies you like, working in batches if necessary, and simply freeze the rest to cook another day – wrap each cookie in parchment to prevent them from sticking together.

4 To cook, line the air-fryer drawer with a sheet of parchment, evenly space however many cookies you want on top, then bake for 14 minutes at 325°F (17 minutes from frozen), or until golden. Transfer to a wire rack, sprinkle with a little extra sugar, if you like, then let cool completely.

5 Snap the chocolate into a heatproof bowl and melt in the air fryer for 2 minutes at 325°F, stir until smooth, then drizzle over the cooled shortbread.

Tip: Stem ginger is well worth seeking out. You'll find it in the international aisle of some grocery stores, or in a specialty store, or online.

ENERGY	FAT	SAT FAT	PROTEIN	CARBS	SUGARS	SALT	FIBER
207kcal	13.4g	8.4g	2.3g	19.8g	6.8g	0g	1.2g

All the bases are covered in this epic

bunch of deliciously sweet treats

Delightful desserts

Cherry chocolate pots

 Serves 6   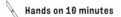 Hands on 10 minutes    Cook 14 minutes, plus cooling   1 Drawer

5 oz dark chocolate (70%)

7 tbsp unsalted butter

¾ cup sugar

3 large eggs

1 small jar of cherries in kirsch

1 Snap the chocolate into a heatproof bowl, cube up and add the butter along with a pinch of sea salt, then melt in the air fryer for 2 to 3 minutes at 325°F. Carefully remove (the bowl will be hot!) and stir to combine.

2 In a separate bowl, whisk the sugar and eggs together until fluffy, then, whisking constantly, pour in the chocolate mixture until combined. Divide between 6 small heatproof teacups or ramekins, then gently push a few cherries into each, pouring the rest, syrup and all, into a small pan for later.

3 Place the cups in the air fryer – in batches if needed – and cook for 12 minutes at 325°F, then carefully remove and let them sit for at least 15 minutes before serving. For maximum pleasure, let them cool to room temperature – if they're hot, they'll be too runny, and if they even touch the fridge, they become too firm. Before serving, place the pan with the cherries over medium heat and reduce the cherry syrup until thick enough for drizzling, then remove. Serve the choc pots with the extra cherries and the reduced syrup. Also wonderful with a spoonful of crème fraîche and an extra grating of chocolate.

Love your freezer

Cover and freeze any uncooked choc pots for another day – they'll keep happily for up to 3 months. Simply cook from frozen for 18 minutes at 325°F, then rest as per step 3 before serving.

ENERGY	FAT	SAT FAT	PROTEIN	CARBS	SUGARS	SALT	FIBER
430kcal	29.3g	17g	6.2g	36.2g	33.7g	0.1g	3.3g

Sweet dressed peaches

 Serves 4   Prep 7 minutes   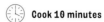 Cook 10 minutes   1 Drawer

4 ripe peaches

½ cup raspberries

½ a lime

1 large sprig of basil

1 heaping tbsp sugar

1 Halve and pit the peaches, then place them cut-side down in the air-fryer drawer and cook for 10 minutes at 400°F, or until soft. As soon as they're cool enough to handle, pinch off and discard the skins.

2 In a bowl, roughly mash the raspberries with a fork, mix in the lime juice, then stir in the peaches to coat. You can eat them warm, like this, or cover and pop into the fridge to chill for up to 3 days.

3 Pick the basil leaves, then use your thumbs and fingertips to rub the leaves into the sugar, making a rough basil sugar to sprinkle over the peaches to serve. Great with ice cream, meringues and yogurt, or sweetened ricotta.

ENERGY	FAT	SAT FAT	PROTEIN	CARBS	SUGARS	SALT	FIBER
51kcal	0.1g	0g	0.9g	12.6g	11.8g	0g	1g

Pineapple tarte Tatin

 Serves 4    Hands on 7 minutes    Cook 39 minutes   1 Drawer

¼ cup sliced almonds

1 x 15-oz can of
pineapple slices in juice

1 oz stem ginger, plus
4 tbsp stem ginger syrup

1 sheet of puff pastry
(about 7 x 9 inches)

3 tbsp unsweetened
shredded coconut

4 scoops of vanilla ice cream

1 Remove the shelf from the air-fryer drawer, scatter in the almonds and cook for 4 minutes at 375°F, or until lightly golden, then remove.

2 Drain the pineapple (save the juice for dressings or marinades) and carefully arrange the slices across the base of the drawer, overlapping and cutting to fit as needed. Drizzle with 2 tablespoons of stem ginger syrup, then thinly slice and sprinkle on the stem ginger. Cook for 20 minutes at 400°F.

3 Gently stretch or roll out the pastry to the size of the drawer. Use tongs to flip the pineapple, then lay the pastry on top, carefully poking and tucking it in at the edges. Cook for 15 minutes at 400°F, or until golden and puffed up.

4 Just before the time's up, place the coconut in a shallow bowl and roll each scoop of ice cream in it to coat. Carefully and confidently flip the tarte Tatin out of the drawer onto a board. Drizzle with the remaining 2 tablespoons of stem ginger syrup, sprinkle with the toasted almonds, cut the tarte into quarters, and top each slice with a scoop of coconut-covered ice cream.

ENERGY	FAT	SAT FAT	PROTEIN	CARBS	SUGARS	SALT	FIBER
390kcal	20.5g	11.1g	6.2g	45.2g	27.4g	0.2g	2.5g

Sensational s'mores

For the ultimate sweet treat, without having to light a fire! My River goes mad for these – if I tell him how easy they are to make in the air fryer, we'd have a problem! Make only if you can operate with self-restraint . . .

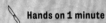 **Hands on 1 minute**   **Cook 3 minutes**   **1 Drawer**

For one single s'more, cut a circle of parchment paper, or if making multiple, you can simply line the air-fryer drawer. Place your **favorite plain biscuits** inside – digestives, graham crackers and gingersnaps all give great results – and place **2 regular or 1 giant marshmallow** on top of each one. Cook for 2 minutes at 350°F, then pull out the drawer and place a square of **dark (70%) or milk chocolate** on top of each gooey marshmallow. Shut the drawer and let the chocolate melt in the residual heat for 15 seconds, then top each stack with another biscuit, flip, let sit for 1 minute and devour!

Stuffed apples

 Serves 4    **Hands on 13 minutes**   **Cook 25 minutes**   **1 Drawer**

4 small apples

¼ cup mixed dried fruit

1 oz drained stem ginger in syrup

¼ cup sliced almonds

2 tbsp demerara sugar

1 pinch of ground cinnamon

4 tbsp soft unsalted butter

4 small slices of fruit bread or brioche

1 Keeping them whole, use an apple corer or a small sharp knife to remove and discard the core of each apple, then use the knife to carefully score around the middle a couple of times, going almost as deep as the core.

2 Finely chop the dried fruit and ginger, transfer to a bowl, add the almonds, sugar, cinnamon and butter, then use your clean hands to massage and mix it all together really well. Poke into the center of the apples, reserving the excess.

3 Evenly space the slices of fruit bread in the air-fryer drawer and place one filled apple on each. Cook for 15 minutes at 325°F.

4 Spoon any extra filling on top of the apples and cook for another 10 minutes at 325°F, or until soft and golden. Serve with hot or cold custard, crème anglaise or ice cream, and enjoy!

ENERGY	FAT	SAT FAT	PROTEIN	CARBS	SUGARS	SALT	FIBER
302kcal	14.3g	7.1g	4.5g	40.4g	26.9g	0.3g	3.3g

Pear & blackberry crumble

 Serves 6    **Hands on 12 minutes**    **Cook 50 minutes**   **1 Drawer**

4 ripe pears

2 apples

2 oz stem ginger, plus
2 tbsp stem ginger syrup

2 cups blackberries

7 tbsp cold unsalted butter

1 large orange

1¼ cups old-fashioned
rolled oats

5 tbsp demerara sugar

1 pinch of ground cinnamon

3 cups cornflakes

1 Cut the pears and apples into sixths, removing and discarding the cores. Finely chop the stem ginger. Remove the shelf from the air fryer, then place the pears, apples, blackberries and ginger inside with ½ tablespoon of butter, the orange zest and juice, and the stem ginger syrup. Mix together and cook for 40 minutes at 350°F, or until the fruit has softened, stirring halfway.

2 Meanwhile, place the oats in a bowl, cube up and add the remaining butter, then rub together with your thumbs and fingertips. Add the sugar and cinnamon, scrunch in the cornflakes, and mix well.

3 Scatter the crumble mixture over the fruit and cook for another 10 minutes at 350°F, or until golden and bubbling, then serve straight from the drawer. Great with custard, crème fraîche or ice cream.

ENERGY	FAT	SAT FAT	PROTEIN	CARBS	SUGARS	SALT	FIBER
378kcal	15.6g	9g	4.3g	58.7g	32.1g	0.2g	5.3g

Eton mess trifle

 Serves 6    Hands on 9 minutes   Cook 15 minutes, plus resting   1 Drawer

unsalted butter, for greasing

5 oz sliced panettone or brioche

1 tbsp sweet sherry or elderflower cordial

1 lb ripe strawberries

½ cup plus 2 tbsp superfine sugar

5 tbsp sliced almonds

2 oz dark chocolate

2 large eggs

1 Remove the shelf from the air-fryer drawer, rub the inside of the drawer with butter, then line with scrunched-up damp parchment paper, keeping the paper away from the heating element. Cover the base with the panettone and drizzle with the sherry.

2 Hull and slice the strawberries, toss with 2 tablespoons of sugar and layer on top. Scatter in the almonds, snap in the chocolate, and cook for 10 minutes at 350°F.

3 Separate the eggs. Put the whites into a bowl (save the yolks in the fridge for another use), add a pinch of sea salt and whisk until the mixture forms stiff peaks – use a handheld mixer, if you've got one. With the mixer still running, gradually add the remaining ½ cup of sugar until glossy and combined, then spoon into the drawer, making peaks with the back of the spoon.

4 Cook for 5 minutes at 375°F, or until golden, then remove the drawer and let sit for 15 minutes to 1 hour (depending on whether you want it warm).

5 Use the parchment to help you lift out the trifle, then slice, divide between bowls and devour! Perfect with hot or cold custard – the choice is yours.

Easy swap

I've used strawberries here, but raspberries, blueberries, blackberries or any other seasonal berries would also work great.

ENERGY	FAT	SAT FAT	PROTEIN	CARBS	SUGARS	SALT	FIBER
277kcal	9.6g	4.6g	5.1g	43.4g	34.5g	0.2g	5.3g

Peach Alaska

 Serves 4   Hands on 12 minutes, plus freezing   Cook 14 minutes, plus resting   🔲 1 Drawer

2 large scoops of
good vanilla ice cream

1 handful of unsalted hazelnuts

2 large eggs

½ cup superfine sugar

1 hot cross bun

sherry or elderflower cordial,
for drizzling

2 tbsp chocolate-
hazelnut spread

½ x 15-oz can of sliced
peaches in juice

1 Ball up 2 nice round scoops of ice cream and place back in the freezer until frozen solid. Put the hazelnuts into the air-fryer drawer and cook for 4 minutes at 375°F, or until lightly golden, then remove.

2 Separate the eggs, putting the whites into a bowl or the bowl of a stand mixer (save the yolks in the fridge for another use). Add a little pinch of sea salt and whisk until the mixture forms stiff peaks, then, with the mixer still running, gradually add the sugar until glossy and combined.

3 Halve the hot cross bun and place on two circles of parchment paper. Drizzle a little sherry over the cut sides, then top with the chocolate spread. Drain the peaches, pat dry well with paper towels, and arrange half on top of each.

4 For the first Alaska, top one of the hot cross bun stacks with a scoop of ice cream, then spoon or pipe on half the meringue mixture, making a few pretty peaks and making sure the ice cream and bun are completely covered.

5 Carefully transfer the Alaska to the drawer, on its paper, and cook for 5 minutes at 375°F, or until the meringue is golden all over.

6 Remove and let sit for 1 to 2 minutes, so the meringue can crisp up slightly. Bash or roughly chop the hazelnuts and sprinkle on top, then slice and serve right away, for sharing. Repeat steps 4 to 6 to make your second Alaska.

Tip: If you can't find hot cross buns, use 1 x 3-inch round of panettone, brioche, sponge cake or pound cake for each Alaska.

Thought that was good? Turn the page for two more delicious combos you can try . . .

ENERGY	FAT	SAT FAT	PROTEIN	CARBS	SUGARS	SALT	FIBER
312kcal	9.8g	3.1g	5.5g	47.5g	42.5g	0.2g	1.7g

Apricot Alaska

Berry ripple ice cream, chopped fruit and nut mix,
fruit bread, brandy, raspberry jam and canned apricots

Mandarin Alaska

Chocolate ice cream, toasted pine nuts, panettone,
Cointreau, marmalade and canned mandarins

Layered vanilla cheesecake

 Serves 8   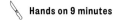 Hands on 9 minutes    Cook 24 minutes, plus cooling   1 Drawer

unsalted butter, for greasing

1¼ lb cream cheese

1⅓ cups confectioner's sugar, plus extra for dusting

1 tbsp vanilla bean paste

3 large eggs

¼ cup all-purpose flour

3½ oz dark chocolate (70%)

½ a blood or regular orange

1 tbsp runny honey

1½ cups raspberries

1 Check that a 6-inch springform pan fits in your air fryer, then lightly grease it and line the bottom with parchment paper.

2 Beat the cream cheese in a large bowl to soften slightly, then sift in the confectioner's sugar, add the vanilla and beat until smooth. One by one, add the eggs, whisking well after each addition. Sift in the flour and beat again.

3 Pour one-third of the mixture into the prepared pan, shake gently to even it out, then place the pan in the drawer and cook for 10 minutes at 400°F.

4 Now snap in half of the chocolate, then pour in half the remaining mixture, smoothing it out to the edges with a spatula. Cook for 7 minutes at 400°F.

5 Next, snap in the rest of the chocolate and pour in the remaining mixture, again smoothing to the edges. Cook for a final 7 minutes at 400°F, then remove and cool to room temperature, or enjoy cold from the fridge.

6 To make the sauce, squeeze the orange juice into a bowl, add the honey, then mash well with half the raspberries, stirring in the remaining whole raspberries just before serving. Loosen the edges of the cheesecake with a knife, then remove, slice and serve with the raspberry sauce.

ENERGY	FAT	SAT FAT	PROTEIN	CARBS	SUGARS	SALT	FIBER
413kcal	26.5g	17g	7.6g	37.6g	33.3g	0.5g	2.3g

Cooking sustainably & kitchen notes

Celebrate quality & seasonality

As is often the case in cooking, using quality ingredients really does make a difference to the success of the recipes. I've tried to keep the number of ingredients under control, so I'm hoping that will give you the excuse to trade up where you can, buying the best veggies, fish or meat you can find. Also, remember that shopping in season always allows your food to be more delicious and more affordable. When it comes to veg and fruit, remember to give everything a nice wash before you start cooking, especially if you're using stuff raw. Ingredients that are noticeably more delicious when you choose the best quality are canned tomatoes, sausages, cheese, beans and chickpeas, crunchy peanut & sesame chili oil, sea salt, honey and chocolate.

Focusing on fish & seafood

Fish and seafood are an incredibly delicious source of protein, but literally the minute they're caught they start to deteriorate in freshness, so you want to buy them as close to the day of your meal as you can – I wouldn't endorse them being stored in the fridge for days; you're better off with frozen if that's the case. I recommend planning your fish and seafood dinners around your shopping days. Make sure you choose responsibly sourced fish and seafood – talk to your fishmonger and take their advice. Try to mix up your choices, choosing seasonal, sustainable options as they're available. If you can only find farmed fish, check that it's responsibly sourced.

Meat & eggs

When it comes to meat, of course I'm going to endorse higher-welfare farming practices, like organic or free-range. Animals should be raised well, free to roam, display natural behaviors and live a stress-free healthy life. Like most things, you pay more for quality. I'm always a believer that if you take a couple of minutes to plan your weekly menus, you can be clever about using cheaper cuts of meat, or you could try cooking some of my meat-reduced and vegetarian dishes, which should give you the opportunity to trade up to quality proteins when you do choose them. For a few of the cuts of meat in this book, you might like to go to a butcher, and I cannot recommend this enough – they can be so helpful: they can order stuff in especially for you and can ensure you have the exact weights you need. Unless essential to a recipe, we don't specify egg sizes. Hens naturally lay a variety of sizes of egg, so look for mixed-size boxes when shopping to support the best possible welfare standards. When it comes to eggs and anything containing eggs, such as pasta or mayo – always choose free-range or organic.

Dial up your dairy

With staple dairy products, like milk, yogurt and butter, please trade up to organic if you can. Unlike meat, it is only slightly more expensive and I couldn't recommend it enough, if it's available to you. Every time you buy organic, you vote for a better food system that supports the highest standards of animal welfare, where both cows and land are well looked after.

Maximizing flavor

In this book I use a lot of what I like to call "flavor bombs": widely available ingredients that allow you to add big bonus flavor, fast. Much-loved pastes include harissa, miso, gochujang, pesto, tahini and many curry pastes. Useful things in brine include jarred roasted red peppers, olives and capers. Helpful things in oil: anchovies and sun-dried tomatoes. These all really bolster the flavor of a dish with just one supercharged ingredient. I love spices and blends like dukkah, curry powder, dried red chili flakes and smoked paprika, to name a few, as well as nuts, seeds and dried fruit; cracking condiments, such as mustards, chili oils and sauces, and mango chutney, as well as super sauces like BBQ, hoisin, soy and fish sauce. They all work so hard on the flavor front. These items guarantee flavor and consistency, educate your palate and save hours of time in preparation. Most are non-perishable, which means you're not under pressure to use them up super-quickly.

Bigging up fresh herbs

Fresh herbs are a gift to any cook. Instead of buying them, why not grow them yourself in the yard or in a pot on your windowsill? Herbs allow you to add single-minded flavor to a dish, without the need to over-season, which is good for everyone. They're also packed with all sorts of incredible qualities on the nutritional front – we like that. And don't forget dried herbs – they're not a compromise for fresh, they're just different.

Wonderfully, they still retain a huge amount of nutritional value, but it's the dramatic change in flavor that is useful to us cooks. Plus, they're non-perishable and super-convenient to have ready and raring to go.

Fridge organization

When juggling space in the fridge, remember that raw meat and fish should be well wrapped and placed on the bottom shelf to avoid cross-contamination. Any food that is ready to eat, whether it's cooked or it doesn't need to be cooked, should be stored on a higher shelf.

The freezer is your best friend

For busy people, without a doubt your freezer, if stocked correctly, is your closest ally. There are just a few basic rules when it comes to really utilizing it well. If you're batch cooking, remember to let food cool thoroughly before freezing – break it down into portions so it cools quicker, and get it into the freezer within 2 hours. Make sure everything is well wrapped, and labeled for future reference. Thaw in the fridge before use, and use within 48 hours. If you've frozen cooked food, don't freeze it again after reheating or defrosting it. Nutritionally speaking, freezing veg and fruit quickly after harvesting retains the nutritional value very efficiently, often trumping fresh equivalents that have been stuck in the supply chain for a while. You will see me using frozen veg and fruit (which I love!) in these recipes – it's super-convenient and widely available.

Air fryer lovin'

All recipes were tested at least twice in a Tefal single (4.2 liters/4.4 quarts) or dual (8.3 liters/8.7 quarts) air fryer, as well as in a range of air fryers by my team of office testers at home. All air fryers are different, so results may vary – please follow the recipe instructions for guidance, and use your instincts to adjust times accordingly if your machine runs a little hotter or colder than average.

A note from Jamie's nutrition team

Our job is to make sure that Jamie can be super-creative, while also ensuring that all recipes meet our guidelines. Every book has a different brief, and *Easy Air Fryer* is about recipes for every day of the week that can be cooked in an air fryer. With the exception of the Delightful Desserts chapter and the hacks, 70% of the recipes fit into our everyday food guidelines. In some cases, recipes aren't complete meals, so you'll need to balance out your menus with what's lacking – the info that follows will help you with this. For clarity and so that you can make informed choices, we've presented easy-to-read nutrition info for each dish on the recipe page (displayed per serving). We also want to inspire a more sustainable way of eating, so 72% of the recipes are either meat-free or meat-reduced (meaning they contain at least 30% less meat than a regular portion size). Food is fun, joyful and creative – it gives us energy and plays a crucial role in keeping our bodies healthy. Remember, a nutritious, varied and balanced diet and regular exercise are the keys to a healthier lifestyle. We don't label foods as "good" or "bad" – there's a place for everything. We encourage an understanding of the difference between nutritious foods for everyday consumption and those to be enjoyed occasionally. For more info about our guidelines and how we analyze recipes, please visit jamieoliver.com/nutrition.

Rozzie Batchelar – Senior Nutritionist, RNutr (food)

A bit about balance

Balance is key when it comes to eating well. Balance your plate right and keep your portion control in check, and you can be confident that you're giving yourself a great start on the path to good health. It's important to consume a variety of foods to ensure we get the nutrients our bodies need to stay healthy. You don't have to be spot-on every day – just try to get your balance right across the week. If you eat meat and fish, as a general guide for main meals, you want at least 2 portions of fish a week, one of which should be oily. Split the rest of the week's main meals between brilliant plant-based meals, some poultry and a little red meat. An all-vegetarian diet can be perfectly healthy, too.

What's the balance?

The UK government's Eatwell Guide shows us what a healthy balance of food looks like. The figures below indicate the proportion of each food group that's recommended across the day.

THE FIVE FOOD GROUPS (UK)	PROPORTION
Vegetables & fruit	40%
Starchy carbohydrates (bread, rice, potatoes, pasta)	38%
Protein (lean meat, fish, eggs, beans, other non-dairy sources)	12%
Dairy foods, milk & dairy alternatives	8%
Unsaturated fats (such as oils)	1%
AND DON'T FORGET TO DRINK PLENTY OF WATER, TOO	

Try to consume foods and drinks high in fat, salt or sugar only occasionally.

Vegetables & fruit

To live a good, healthy life, vegetables and fruit should sit right at the heart of your diet. Veg and fruit come in all kinds of colors, shapes, sizes, flavors and textures, and contain different vitamins and minerals, which each play a part in keeping our bodies healthy and optimal, so variety is key. Eat the rainbow, mixing up your choices as much as you can and embracing the seasons so you're getting produce at its best and its most nutritious. As an absolute minimum, aim for at least 5 portions of fresh, frozen or canned veg and fruit every day of the week, enjoying more wherever possible. 80g/3 oz (or a large handful) counts as 1 portion. You can also count one 30g/1 oz portion of dried fruit, one 80g/3 oz portion of beans or pulses, and 150ml/2/3 cup of unsweetened veg or fruit juice per day.

Starchy carbohydrates

Carbs provide us with a large proportion of the energy needed to make our bodies move, and to ensure our organs have the fuel they need to function. When you can, choose fiber-rich whole grain and whole wheat varieties. 260g/9 oz is the recommended daily amount of carbohydrates for the average adult, with up to 90g/3 oz coming from total sugars, which includes natural sugars found in whole fruit, milk and milk products, and no more than 30g/1 oz of free sugars. Free sugars are those added to food and drink, including sugar found in honey, syrups, fruit juice and smoothies. Fiber is classified as a carbohydrate and is mainly found in plant-based foods such as whole grains, veg and fruit. It helps to keep our digestive systems healthy, control our blood-sugar levels and maintain healthy cholesterol levels. Adults should be aiming for at least 30g/1 oz of fiber each day.

Protein

Think of protein as the building blocks of our bodies – it's used for everything that's important to how we grow and repair. Try to vary your proteins to include more beans and pulses, two sources of sustainably sourced fish per week (one of which is oily) and reduce red and processed meat if your diet is high in these. Choose lean cuts of animal-based protein where you can. Beans, peas and lentils are great alternatives to meat because they're naturally low in fat and, as well as protein, they contain fiber and some vitamins and minerals. Other nutritious protein sources include tofu, eggs, nuts and seeds. Variety is key! The requirement for an average woman aged 19 to 50 is 45g/1½ oz per day, with 55g/2 oz for men in the same age bracket.

Dairy foods, milk & dairy alternatives

This food group offers an amazing array of nutrients when eaten in the right amounts. Favor organic dairy milk and yogurt, and small amounts of cheese, in this category; the lower-fat varieties (with no added sugar) are equally brilliant and worth embracing. If opting for plant-based versions, I think it's great that we have choice, but it's really important to look for unsweetened fortified options that have added calcium, iodine and vitamin B12 in the ingredients list, to avoid missing out on the key nutrients provided by dairy milk.

Unsaturated fats

While we only need small amounts, we do require healthier fats. Choose unsaturated sources where you can, such as olive and liquid vegetable oils, nuts, seeds, avocado and omega-3 rich oily fish. Generally speaking, it's recommended that the average woman has no more than 70g/2½ oz of fat per day, with less than 20g/¾ oz of that from saturated fat, and the average man no more than 90g/3 oz, with less than 30g/1 oz from saturated fat.

Drink plenty of water

To be the best you can be, stay hydrated. Water is essential to life, and to every function of the human body! In general, women aged 14 and over need at least 2 liters/8 cups per day, and men in the same age bracket need at least 2.5 liters/10 cups per day.

Energy & nutrition info

The average woman needs 2,000 calories per day, while the average man needs roughly 2,500. These figures are a rough guide, and what we eat needs to be considered in relation to factors like your age, build, lifestyle and activity levels.

Big thanks

Ah, the thanks page. Tucked away at the back of every book, this little double-page spread is actually really rather important, as it contains the names of all those wonderfully talented and committed people who support me in the creation of my books. From the very inception of an idea to the physical book you hold in your hands right now, a multitude of clever brains help me to shape and hone the content, to physically create it, and of course, to get it out to all of you. Inevitably I'll forget someone here, so please forgive me if that's you, and know that I appreciate you endlessly.

First up, the mighty food team, who help me develop the recipes and identify any gaps, who test, test, test the recipes to make sure they really work, and who support me in the photo shoots that fill these pages with visual joy and inspiration. Led with gusto by the formidable and divine Ginny Rolfe, the team also includes lovely and talented Joss Herd, Ben Slater, Anna Helm Baxter and Rachel Young, as well as the amazing

Sharon Sharpe. Big respect to Laura McLeish for keeping us organized, as well as wonderful Helen Martin (I hope you have your feet up with a glass of something delicious when you read this – happy retirement!). Huge admiration for my right-hand foodie friends, Pete Begg and Bobby Sebire, you know I love you. I'm also lucky to have some incredibly loyal and talented freelance food teamers. Thank you to top testers Isla Murray and Maddie Rix, and to Sophie Mackinnon, Fran Paling and Eliot Burke on this one.

Doing her thing with patience and grace on the nutrition front is my Senior Nutritionist Rozzie Batchelar. And keeping us in check when it comes to food safety, standards, farming and ethics is Lucinda Cobb.

Steering the ship and taking care of the words is my wonderful Editor-in-Chief Rebecca Verity, supported by brilliant Jade Melling and the queen of air-fryer testing, Ruth Tebby, as well as Polly Mackintosh and the rest of my ace editorial team.

Over on design and all things creative, much respect to my main man, Creative Director James Verity, and to lovely Davina Mistry and the rest of the brilliant design team.

I'm really in love with the fresh, clean look of the photography in this one, and that is down to my dear friend and respected photographer, Mr David Loftus, supported buoyantly by Richard Bowyer.

On to my publishers, the powerhouse that is Penguin Random House. Many of the team have been part of this wonderful world of publishing with me for a lot of years now, and I'm ever so grateful for that constancy. To my great friend Tom Weldon, and the always stylish Louise Moore. To Elizabeth Smith, Clare Parker, Tom Troughton, Ella Watkins, Rebecca Ogden, Juliette Butler, Katherine Tibbals, Lee Motley, Sarah Fraser, Nick Lowndes, Christina Ellicott, Emily Harvey, Kelly Mason, Eleanor Rhodes Davies, Emma Carter, Hannah Padgham, Chris Wyatt, Tracy Orchard, Chantal Noel, Anjali Nathani, Kate Reiners, Tyra Burr, Joanna Whitehead, Agnes Watters, Lee-Anne Williams, Jessica Meredeen, Danielle Appleton, Grace Dellar, Sally Hargrave, Stuart Anderson, Anna Curvis, Akua Akowuah, Samantha Waide, Richard Rowlands and Carrie Anderson.

And love as always for dear Annie Lee, for Emma Horton, Jill Cole and Catherine Hookway.

My team at JO HQ are a wonderful bunch of passionate, talented people who I'm lucky enough to work with on a daily basis. They all throw their enthusiasm and creativity at every book. Calling out some key players here, thank you to marketing maestros Rosalind Godber and Clare Duffy, and the queens of PR Tamsyn Zeitsman and Lydia Waller. To the social crew led by Letitia Becher, to Rich Herd and the rest of the VPU. To very important Pamela Lovelock, Therese MacDermott and dear John Dewar, and to Timiko Cranwell and the legal gang. Of course there are many other brilliant teams, including personnel, operations, IT, P&D and facilities.

Extra special mention to my CEO, Mr Kevin Styles, to my long-standing deputy Louise Holland, to my mighty Media MD Zoe Collins, and the very best EA I could wish for, Ali Solway.

And a big, big thank-you to my incredible team of office testers who willingly volunteer to cook up the recipes at home in their own time and give lots of useful and insightful feedback to help me make the recipes as reliable as possible.

Over on the TV front, there's always a lot of wonderful people to shout about, but here I'm focusing on the long-standing team. To the trio of dreams, Sean Moxhay, Sam Beddoes and Katie Millard, thank you for your commitment and determination. Thank you also to Amanda Doig-Moore, Renzo Luzardo, Prarthana Peterarulthas and the rest of the amazing crew from the TV show. Big love for my brother Tobie Tripp on the tunes. And respect as always for Tim Hancock and all the team at Channel 4, and to the wonderful gang over at Fremantle.

Julia Bell, you know what you mean to me, thank you for what you do.

And saving the best for last, all the love for my ever-supportive, funny, chaotic, brilliant family. To my darling Jools, to my beautiful girls Pops, Daisy and Petal, and my little mates Buddy and River. You all make me so proud. To Mum and Dad, my guiding lights, to the rest of the fam, and to the don, the one and only Gennaro Contaldo, one day, my friend, I'll show you how an air fryer works . . .

Index

Recipes marked **V** are suitable for vegetarians; in some instances you'll need to swap in a vegetarian alternative to cheese such as Parmesan.

S

For a quick reference list of all the vegetarian, vegan, dairy-free and gluten-free recipes in this book, visit jamieoliver.com/easyairfryer/reference

The Jamie Oliver collection

Hungry for more?

For handy nutrition advice, as well as videos, features, hints, tricks and tips on all sorts of different subjects, loads of brilliant recipes, plus much more, check out

JAMIEOLIVER.COM   #EASYAIRFRYER

Photography by David Loftus

Designed by Jamie Oliver Limited

Color reproduction by Altaimage Ltd

jamieoliver.com

www.flatironbooks.com

The Library of Congress Cataloging-in-Publication Data is available upon request.

ISBN 978-1-250-39797-3 (paper over board)
ISBN 978-1-250-39798-0 (ebook)

Our books may be purchased in bulk for promotional, educational, or business use. Please contact your local bookseller or the Macmillan Corporate and Premium Sales Department at 1-800-221-7945, extension 5442, or by email at MacmillanSpecialMarkets@macmillan.com.

Originally published in the United Kingdom in 2025 by Penguin Michael Joseph, part of the Penguin Random House group of companies

First U.S. Edition: 2025

Printed in China

10   9   8   7   6   5   4   3   2   1

Big love

Thank you for buying my cookbook – by
doing so you're contributing to my Ministry
of Food Programme, which is on a mission
to teach 1 million people to cook by 2030.

FIND OUT MORE:
JAMIEOLIVER.COM/MOF